The Art Museums of New England

The Art Museums of New England

New Hampshire, Vermont & Maine

S. Lane Faison, Jr.

David R. Godine · Publisher · Boston

This edition first published in 1982 by
David R. Godine, Publisher, Inc.
306 Dartmouth Street
Boston, Massachusetts 02116

Library of Congress Cataloging in Publication Data
Faison, Samson Lane, 1907-
    The art museums of New England.

    (Godine guides ; 3)
    First ed. (1958) published under title: A guide to the art museums of New England.
    Includes index.
    1. Art museums—New England—Guide-books.
2. Art—New England—Guide-books.   I.   Title.
N510.5.N4F2   1982   708.14   80-83952
ISBN 0-87923-372-9
ISBN 0-87923-373-7 (pbk.)

This is a revised and expanded version of Mr. Faison's *Guide to the Art Museums of New England*, published in 1958 by Harcourt, Brace & Co.

Manufactured in the United States of America

Gratefully dedicated to the directors and staff members of the institutions here surveyed, and to hospitable friends along the road

Contents

Maine

How to Use This Book

The survey of museum collections is arranged south to north by states, Connecticut to Maine, and alphabetically by towns within each state. It comes in two forms: a complete hardcover volume that covers all six states and three individual softcover volumes, one for Connecticut and Rhode Island, the second for Massachusetts, and the third for New Hampshire, Vermont, and Maine. Each of the four volumes has an index. The complete hardcover volume is paged consecutively; the separate paperback volumes are paged consecutively as the complete volume is paged: Connecticut and Rhode Island from page 1 to page 111, Massachusetts from page 113 to page 358, and the northern three states from page 359 to page 463.

The map that introduces each state is dotted to indicate proper locations. Each location refers to an adjacent identification list in alphabetical order, which will allow you to turn to the appropriate entry in the main text. In planning a tour these maps should be helpful.

A major feature of the book is a network of cross references to examples in other museums related to the work under discussion. Each reference is therefore followed by a number in parentheses, indicating first the state where the item appears, then the item number. For example, the Degas pastel at the Hill-Stead Museum in Farmington, Conn. (CT 3) is placed in a larger critical and historical context by reference to other works of Degas in the museums of Boston (MA 81), Northampton (MA 179), and Providence (RI 18).

Rather than appending a bibliography, which in a book of this kind would be either too long or much too short to be useful, I have included occasional references to books and articles in the text itself. These are for the general, but curious, reader. The scholar will understand their introductory purpose, and pass on.

Preface

This work surveys, critically and historically, some 550 works of art selected from the *permanent* collections of over one hundred art museums, historical societies, and libraries open to the public in the six New England states.

While the text is directed to the general reader, I have reason to believe that the scholar, too, will be surprised to learn what artistic riches exist in out-of-the-way places. Over twenty years ago, when I first undertook such a survey, I had little idea that sixty institutions would fall within its scope. Since then, many of those originally covered have doubled in size, twenty-four new ones have been established, and eighteen others have subsequently developed collections worthy of inclusion or were originally omitted through oversight.

My earlier book, published in 1958 by Harcourt, Brace and Company under the title *A Guide to the Art Museums of New England*, went out of print within six years. So it has remained, but in the meantime I have filed away corrections and additions in the hope that an updated version would someday be forthcoming. This happy event took place when David Godine, in search of an author for such a book, discovered mine in limbo. He had recently published *New England Gardens Open to the Public*, by Rolce Redard Payne, as the second in a projected series of all–New England handbooks (the first, *The Boston Basin Bicycle Book*, was published in 1975). The present book now becomes the third; it is to be followed by a comparable volume, *A Guide to Historic Houses of New England Open to the Public*, by Margaret Supplee Smith and R. Jackson Smith.

The word "guide" has been eliminated in the new title because it suggests a purely descriptive compilation à la Baedeker, whereas I propose an excursion into art criticism and art history based on the vast treasure available to the public in New England. Some of the present text repeats selections and comments in the older one. While masterpieces of art are not quite so dependable as the heavenly bodies, and in the interim connoisseurship has reduced the magnitude of a few of them, for the most part the original text has been greatly expanded rather than cut. Everywhere it has been corrected, refined, or reoriented as the case seemed to demand.

Twenty-odd years ago I did not suspect that even if the Boston Museum of Fine Arts were eliminated, the whole range of world art—from antiquity to the present, and from Western art to Far Eastern, Pre-Columbian, and so-called primitive art—would still be abundantly represented in fine original examples in New England's museums. Today, if we leave out of account the world's great metropolitan centers, it is fair to say that no region of comparable size anywhere can boast such a concentration of art museums as New England. Yet the area of the six New England states is about the size of Oklahoma and less than a third of that of France, and under one-sixth of France's size if we subtract the museumless expanses of hinterland Maine. Even more extraordinary is the concentration in Massachusetts alone—an area just half the size of Denmark. Almost half the museums and nearly three-fifths of the works of art surveyed here are in the Bay State.

Arranged south to north state by state, this is not a book to be read in the usual sequence. The informed student of art will find what is wanted by consulting the table of contents or the index; these will lead to quick answers as to what is to be seen in any given institution, or which of them have significant examples (cited in these pages) of the work of a given artist or of types of art, such as African, Chinese, or Pre-Columbian. The general reader who wishes to get an overview of the development of art history might well start with the section on the Boston Museum of Fine Arts. This provides a kind of miniature survey of Western art, and it contains the book's most significant coverage of Far Eastern art. Less comprehensive surveys will be found in the sections on other leading museums. The fullest discussion of primitive art is contained in the entry on the Peabody Museum at Harvard University.

In a selective project of this sort, injustices inevitably occur. For omissions and misplaced emphases I can only ask the reader's indulgence. Some explanation, however, is necessary for the treatment of historical societies and libraries. As the number of these in New England is very large, it was possible to include only those that own works of art of consequence, or more modest ones that interestingly supplement the discussion of works commented on elsewhere. The exclusion of such an institution is in no way to be taken as a judgment of its intrinsic eminence.

The total of some 550 works illustrated and discussed is a compromise between the claims of broad coverage and portable size. *Portable*: a book to be carried with you into the museum and, it is hoped, read in the presence of the original works of art. *Coverage*: this or any other total could easily have been devoted to the Boston Museum of Fine Arts alone. While it was obvious from the start that B M F A should receive more emphasis than any other, it became equally obvious that to allow the total for all the museums of Boston and Cambridge to exceed a quarter of the selections for the whole book would mean eliminating many small museums elsewhere. (As it has worked out, Boston and Cambridge are represented by 128 works, or about 23 percent of the whole.) Smaller places contain works that are worth a pilgrimage; and the experience of traveling to see a fine object becomes part of the experience the object itself can provide. I do not mean that you will come upon a Chartres Cathedral or an Arena Chapel in rural New England, but who could wish that these shrines were in Paris or Florence? In somewhat the same way a watercolor, a precious ivory, or a superb impression of a Rembrandt etching, suddenly come upon in a small museum, or a modest painting by a hitherto unfamiliar artist, can have a greater effect than if the same work were seen—or very possibly missed —in a major institution.

The reader will discover, with a few exceptions in the case of prints, that furniture, photographs, and prints are not discussed in these pages.

The same holds true, again with a few exceptions, for the decorative arts in general. This policy was dictated by limitations of space and by the theory that all these arts are "multiples," in the broad sense that identical or nearly identical examples are usually to be found in several institutions. Where it is appropriate, however, reference is made to important collections of decorative arts, furniture, photographs, and prints.

Visitors are warned not to expect that my selections (often made from works in storage) will always be on display, museum by museum, to welcome them. Shortage of exhibition space often dictates a policy of rotation, and temporary shows can mean that whole galleries have to be cleared and their contents stored. Loans to other museums can account for other absentees, yet there is an extra dividend of pleasure in finding a work in unexpected surroundings and new contexts.

Within the limits defined above, each entry attempts a selection of what is outstanding in the museum under discussion. On many occasions you will naturally question why certain works were not included. There are many answers, and I will leave to your judgment which of the following are appropriate: (1) limitations of space in the book; (2) discussion of a generally similar work in some other museum; (3) too many works by the same artist to warrant inclusion of yet another one; (4) poor condition of the work in question; (5) attribution of the work to the given artist doubtful; or, finally, (6) my opinion of it less enthusiastic than yours.

Two pairs of terms frequently appearing in these pages seem to require explanation. By *classical*, I mean pertaining to the art of Greece and Rome. By *classic*, I mean characterized by such restraint, high idealism, and formal discipline as is found in Greek art of the fifth century B.C., in Chinese art of the T'ang dynasty, in Gothic sculpture of the thirteenth century, in the painting of Raphael and Titian and Poussin, and in the nineteenth-century painting of Corot, Cézanne (especially in the 1880s), and Seurat. I hope I have used these terms consistently.

The second pair of terms is *size* and *scale*. By *size*, I mean physical dimensions. By *scale*, I mean the size that the work *seems to suggest*, irrespective of its actual measurements. In this connection, Viollet-le-Duc pointed out in his *Dictionnaire Raisonné de l'Architecture* that although Notre Dame in Paris is approximately the same height as the Arc de Triomphe, the former is scaled to human beings and does not dwarf the neighboring houses; whereas the latter—scaled, we might say, to Napoleon's ambition—is restrained by no such modesty. Contrariwise, a self-portrait in the Louvre by the fifteenth-century French painter Jean Fouquet, painted in gold enamel on a black ground, seems to expand to life size even though this little roundel measures only 3 inches in diameter. It was once attached to the frame of a small two-paneled altarpiece.

Before acknowledging my indebtedness to many kindly persons, I am happy to add a concluding word about the present state of admission fees to art museums in New England and elsewhere in the United States. Many make no charge whatever. When fees are imposed they are modest indeed as compared with the cost of concert or theater tickets, or with golf or ski-tow charges. Free or not, museums often provide a prominently displayed opportunity for the visitor to make a contribution. The need for such support is both real and pressing.

In each of the institutions discussed in these pages, staff members have been generous in providing information, advising me in my choice of works, and in supplying photographs. Many friends along the road have housed and entertained my wife and me, and made our more than four thousand miles of New England travel the more enjoyable. A list of all these benevolent people would inevitably be so long as to defeat its purpose. The book itself is therefore dedicated to them *en masse*. In so doing we hope they will understand that no such screen of collective anonymity clouds our grateful memories of kindnesses received.

Vivian Patterson, a graduate student in the Williams College / Clark Art Institute Master of Arts Program in the History of Art, has been enormously helpful as my research assistant and amanuensis-without-portfolio. The sections on the two museums in Williamstown are in large part her work.

It has been a continuing delight to work with David Godine, my publisher, and William B. Goodman, his editorial director. Their enthusiastic collaboration in my task is warmly appreciated.

The original text and thereby the present one owe much to the cultivated mind and eye of my friend, the late Professor John McAndrew, a former director of the Wellesley College Museum. For scholarly assistance in Rhode Island, I am indebted to my friend Winslow Ames, a distinguished collector and art historian. I must especially thank Cornelius Vermeule, Curator of Classical Art at the Boston Museum of Fine Arts, for extensive and sustained support, not only within and beyond the confines of the museum itself, but also beyond his professional field.

Colleagues in the Williams College Department of Art have given generously of their time and expert knowledge and have saved me many a slip. If flaws remain despite all the assistance outlined above, or if my critical estimates sometimes seem eccentric, the *culpa* is *mea*.

Finally, there is the problem of thanking my wife adequately for her participation in this venture. In truth she is all but the joint author of this book. It is *not* true that without her it would have been written sooner—as occasional dedications have slyly suggested.

> S. Lane Faison, Jr.
> *Director Emeritus*
> *Williams College Museum of Art*

Williamstown, Mass.
October 15, 1981

New Hampshire

New Hampshire

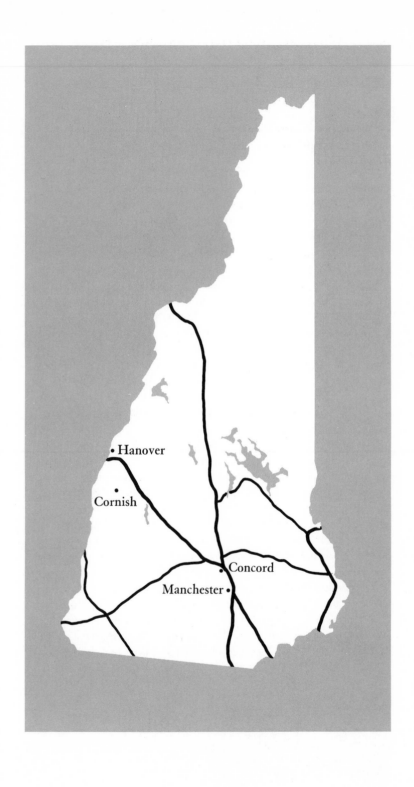

New Hampshire Historical Society

Location: 30 Park Street at State Street (near the state capitol)
Hours: Mon., Tues., Thurs., Fri. 9-4:30, Wed. 9-8 P.M.
Admission: Free

Centered under the elaborate marble entrance-rotunda is a superb example of Concord's famed product, the *Concord Coach*.[1] I hope no one will object to my including it as a work of art—or to my making an exception in its favor in a book that does not cover crafts or manufactured objects. Such coaches were first built by Abbot and Downing, of Concord, from 1827. The example seen here dates from 1852 and was acquired by the Historical Society just over a century later. It was built by J. S. and E. A. Abbot; as the inscription makes clear, it was used by the U.S. Mail. Concord coaches ran in regular service as late as 1910. Up to twelve passengers could be carried inside (in the large models) and as many more seated on the roof. They were also used on the Wells-Fargo routes in the Old West. The society owns a painting showing thirty of them on flatcars being shipped by rail to Omaha, Nebraska, on April 15, 1868. This fascinating picture is by John Burgum (1826–1907), better known as Abbot and Downing's most renowned painter of the coaches themselves.

The society's collection of furniture and paintings (primarily portraits) is important, as are its historical prints and photographs and its research library. Temporary exhibitions are shown in a large gallery to the right of the rotunda. Upstairs is a series of period rooms covering New England life primarily from 1700 to 1750. While there are some historical discrepancies, the representation of household articles and decorative arts is extensive. Painted floors often substituted for carpets, and the black-and-white diamond pattern seen here—imitating marble floors of more affluent homes—was especially popular.

The furniture collection is celebrated among connoisseurs. Among the prize pieces is a high chest of drawers attributed to John Dunlap of New Hampshire, c. 1780. On the grand staircase you cannot miss the full-length *Portrait of Benning Wentworth* by Joseph Blackburn, painted in Portsmouth in 1760. We have discussed a work of this master in a

I

very different vein at Bowdoin College (ME 11). A replica of the portly Governor Wentworth (1696–1770) hangs in the nearby state capitol among its array of gubernatorial images. A companion portrait by Blackburn, also painted in 1760, of *Lieutenant Governor John Wentworth*, who died in 1730, likewise confronts you on the staircase of the Historical Society.

Of wider-ranging historical interest is the *Portrait of Benjamin Thompson, Count Rumford* (1753–1814), in the officer's uniform of the King's American Dragoons, c. 1782. The former attribution of this picture to Thomas Gainsborough has not stood up to modern connoisseurship, particularly when it is compared with the Fogg Art Museum's sparkling image of him (in red coat), unquestionably by that great English master. A Tory sympathizer, Thompson departed from America in 1776 to join the British forces, leaving his wife and an infant daughter. A brilliant scientist, he soon became a member of the Royal Society in London. He commanded British troops in Charleston and on Long Island. After the defeat of the British, in 1783 he traveled to Munich, where he was welcomed by Charles Theodore, Elector of Bavaria. Here he laid out the now famous English Garden, in 1790. Already knighted by King George III, he was now made a Count of the Holy Roman Empire. For his personal title Thompson took the old name of Concord (Rumford), where he had been married. In the following year his wife died in America and by 1796 his daughter Sarah, now twenty-two, had joined him. She so charmed the Elector that he received her as Countess of the Empire, and she was known thereafter as Countess Rumford. It is recorded that, noticing her father's attentions to the young daughter of Countess Baumgarten, and further noticing Sophy's "striking resemblance" to her father, she became aware for the first time that "I was no longer to consider myself an only child." Back in London, Rumford busied himself with a variety of scientific inventions. Settling in Paris in 1803, he courted and married the widow of the guillotined Lavoisier (see MA 239), but the union proved unhappy. His daughter Sarah, who died in 1852, spent her last years at Concord in the home of her birth. Her possessions came to the Historical Society in 1978 through the will of a collateral member of her mother's family. So ends the extraordinary Rumford saga. An exhibition utilizing these memorabilia was organized by the society in 1979; the notes that accompanied it make fascinating reading.

St. Paul's School

Location: Follow Pleasant St. (Route 103) for about 3 miles west of the center of Concord; look for sign on the left for entrance to the school

Hours: Tues.-Sat. 10-4:30 except during school holidays

Admission: Free. Ⓗ

Visible on the grounds near Memorial Hall from April through October, but dismantled and stored during the winter months for safety's sake, is a fine mobile-on-stabile by Alexander Calder (1898–1976). Its playful title, *Iguana*,[2] stretches the imagination a bit, but humor is no stranger to Calder's art, as visitors to the Whitney Museum in New York discover daily in observing the antics of his many-peopled *Circus*. An early mobile of Calder's, rather shrublike in shape, bears the title *Calderberry Bush*. From our visit to Hartford (CT 35) we know that he could rise to the occasion of inventing his own gigantic, but engaging, horse to suit the requirements of a much earlier bequest. In *Iguana*, made in 1968 of aluminum and steel and reaching a height of over 6 feet, the forms and their gay colors relate, as so often, to those of the paintings of Joan Miró (see CT 32). A smaller Calder mobile can be seen in Memorial Hall itself, suspended from the lobby ceiling.

For a good many generations in the history of this distinguished academy, interest in art was restricted to fine buildings (the chapel is an example) and to memorials. One of the latter, in a small oratory to the left of the chapel's entrance, is especially interesting. It is a carefully made replica of the great fresco by Pietro Lorenzetti (Sienese, active 1320–48) in the Lower Church of San Francesco at Assisi, representing the *Madonna and Child with Saints Francis and John the Evangelist.* Commissioned from Nicholas Lochoff, a specialist in this kind of reproduction, it is painted in true fourteenth-century fresco technique (with the gold leaf and certain colors and details added after the plaster had dried). What we see here is a scholarly craftsman's estimate of the appearance of this marvelously expressive work when it was new. Lochoff received another commission, from the Frick Art Reference Library,

2

New York, to make a replica of the same fresco in its modern damaged state. It adorns the main reading room of that institution. To make it, Lochoff produced a work similar to the fresco at St. Paul's and then painstakingly destroyed it to match its twentieth-century condition. Since fresco is made by layers—dry painting atop pigments that have sunk into the wet plaster—you cannot make a satisfactory replica by imitating surfaces in a single medium.

With the considerable growth of concern for art at St. Paul's in the past twenty years, Hargate Hall has been adapted to serve as what is known as The Art Center in Hargate. Excellent exhibitions have been organized, and visits by leading artists, such as Robert Motherwell (see MA 229) in 1970. A taped record of his remarks has been published by the school under the title *On the Humanism of Abstraction*. It is an important statement. A small permanent collection, primarily of American art, is being developed.

Saint-Gaudens National Historic Site

Location: On Route 12A (N.H. side of the Connecticut River), 2 miles north of the covered bridge from Windsor, Vt.; follow the sign up the hill. From Route 91 use exit 8 or 9 toward Windsor

Hours: 8:30-5 daily from the last weekend in May to October 15

Admission: Charged (sixteen years and older)

Operated since 1964 by the National Park Service, the former home and Little Studio of Augustus Saint-Gaudens (1848–1907) have been supplemented by a well-designed gallery and sculpture court where much of his work is shown in originals, models, or casts. The house was once a tavern, built in 1800. The Little Studio was Saint-Gaudens's workshop. A Large Studio, where major works were built to full scale, formerly occupied the site of the gallery, but it burned in 1904 with the loss of Saint-Gaudens's correspondence, sketchbooks, records of commissions, and numerous works in progress. Reconstructed in the following year, it burned again in 1944.

Since American sculpture lagged well behind European work until the late nineteenth century, it may be significant that our greatest sculptor prior to the advent of modern art was born in Dublin of Irish and French parents. He arrived in this country when they emigrated. Like the painter William Michael Harnett (see MA 220), also born in 1848, he was trained at the Cooper Union and the National Academy of Design in New York. For both artists study in Europe was of the highest importance, but there all similarity ends.

The *Diana*,[3] shown in our illustration in its central position in the commodious Little Studio, is a bronze cast of the half-size model for a 13-foot figure that once topped Stanford White's Madison Square Garden in New York (at Fifth Avenue and Twenty-sixth Street, destroyed 1925). The figure itself, installed in 1893 and once gilded, is now at the head of the main staircase of the Philadelphia Museum of Art. Small bronze replicas, with a much less elaborate bow, were sold in some

3

quantity, and may be seen at the Currier Gallery of Art in Manchester, the Williams College Museum of Art, and elsewhere. The half-size bronze at Cornish is actually a cast made in 1972 from the plaster, still preserved at Cornish and the only piece salvaged from the fire of 1944. An earlier bronze cast is in the Metropolitan Museum of Art, New York. A cement cast was presented to Stanford White in 1894, and is now privately owned in New Mexico. In a newspaper interview of 1897 with the young woman who posed for the *Diana*, it was revealed that the pose was so difficult that she had to be propped up by ladders, but the sculptor was so impatient that he made a casting directly from her body. We are not to suppose, however, that he did not make his own alterations and refinements. Saint-Gaudens's cast of a fifth-century B.C. Greek stele, hung in his studio, suggests his concern with Greek idealization at its noblest period rather than with the prevalent taste for smoothed-out Neo-Classicism that had so long held American sculpture in its chill grasp.

Saint-Gaudens's first major commission, which assured his future, came in 1876, for the monument to Admiral David G. Farragut in New York's Madison Square. The plaster for the figure was exhibited in Paris in 1880, where it received an honorable mention, and was cast there in bronze. Erected the following year, it was set on a Hudson River bluestone base. This *Base*,[4] removed in 1934 because of erosion, was replaced by a simple black granite one; it is now a major possession of the Cornish Site. Measuring 7 feet in height by more than 8 in width, it was almost certainly cut by the artist himself, the budget being a tight one and Saint-Gaudens not yet in a position to surround himself with assistants. It is remarkable for a flowing design that can without exaggeration be called Art Nouveau before its time. The long inscription commemorating Farragut is noteworthy for its innovative lettering. A symbolic sword plunges through the central panel of waves, flanked by allegorical figures of Courage (on the right) and Loyalty. These are already marked by a surprising break with Neo-Classical formulae. The whole base forms a semicircular exedra, or seat—again a radical departure from the normal conception of such supports. It is known that Stanford White had much to do with this design; indeed, White signed the base as architect after Saint-Gaudens's signature as sculptor.

Important commissions that followed the enthusiastic reception of the Farragut Monument included *The Puritan* for Springfield, Mass. (MA 209), the Adams Memorial in Rock Creek Cemetery, Washington, D.C.

4

(bronze replica in the garden near the Little Studio), the monument to Colonel Robert G. Shaw (Boston Common opposite the statehouse, earlier full-size design in plaster at Cornish), the General Sherman Monument in New York's Fifty-ninth Street Plaza, and the *Diana* for Madison Square Garden.

Saint-Gaudens settled in Cornish in 1885. Many other artists joined him in the area, including such painters as George de Forest Brush, Thomas Dewing, Kenyon Cox (page 429), Charles Platt (also a distinguished architect), Stephen Parrish, and Stephen's enormously popular son, Maxfield Parrish. Thus the Cornish Colony came into being. It also attracted poets (Witter Bynner), novelists (Winston Churchill), editors, actors, and musicians. The artistic impact of summers at Cornish was great, but it inevitably fell victim to the rising tide of modern art.

We should append to this list of Eminent Victorians (and Edwardians) the sculptor Daniel Chester French (1850–1931), established luxuriously on his own estate at Stockbridge, Mass. (see MA 223). The current revival of all these artists has restored them to their rightful and prestigious place in American art.

Hood Museum of Art, Dartmouth College

Hours: Galleries in the Hopkins Center: Mon.-Fri. 10-4, Sat., Sun. 2-4; Carpenter Hall: Mon.-Fri. 11-4, Sat., Sun. 12-4; Wilson Hall: Mon.-Fri. 9-5, Sat., Sun. 12-4. Holiday hours usually follow Sun. hours, and all galleries closed Christmas and New Year's Day
Admission: Free.

The art collections of Dartmouth College are extensive, but until present hopes for an adequate museum are fulfilled, it is difficult to see them with any completeness. The Hood Museum is scheduled to open in 1984, in a location near the Hopkins Center.

As of this writing, the greater part of the collection is kept in the excellent storage facilities in the basement of Hopkins Center, where the museum offices are also located. Changing selections are shown in two galleries in the center (when they are not occupied by temporary exhibitions) and in Carpenter Hall, a wing off the Baker and Sherman libraries. The archaeological and ethnological collections are displayed in Wilson Hall, across the street left of the main entrance to Hopkins Center. Orozco's impressive fresco cycle fills the walls of a study area below the main floor of the Baker Library. Modern sculptures are placed on the college grounds, in the lobby of Hopkins Center, and in a small court at the center. Carpenter Hall is the home of art history; Wilson Hall, of anthropology; and Hopkins Center, of studio instruction. A college map is available, and most helpful.

Apart from the examples we discuss or mention, Dartmouth owns fine collections of photographs, prints of all periods (especially rich in Piranesi, nineteenth-century masters, and among the very few American museums to own the complete Vollard suite of 100 etchings by Picasso), posters from both world wars, and Chinese porcelains. There are also collections of coins and medals, and of costumes.

Among New England colleges that received Assyrian reliefs during the mid-nineteenth century through the interest of missionary alumni, Dartmouth and Amherst received the lion's share. These reliefs are discussed in the entry for Amherst College (MA 1), but to Dartmouth belongs the credit for a publication of its group (in relation to the more than seventy in American museums) in a brochure by John B. Stearns and Donald P. Hanson, *The Assyrian Reliefs at Dartmouth* (1953).

Art collecting at Dartmouth began in 1771 with the presentation of a silver bowl of "monteith" type by Colonial Governor John Wentworth, a trustee of the institution. It was made in Boston by Daniel Henchman and Nathaniel Hurd, two of Paul Revere's most highly considered competitors. Dartmouth's first painting, which hangs in the Baker Library, is a full-length *Portrait of Eleazar Wheelock III* (1711-79), the college's first president, commissioned in 1793 from Joseph Steward. Later portraits with Dartmouth connections include works by Chester Harding and Thomas Sully. An important gift of over one hundred paintings and including bronze sculptures by Georg Kolbe and Charles Despiau was received from Mrs. John D. Rockefeller, Jr., in 1935. Primarily by living American painters, the works also included Thomas Eakins's *Portrait of the Architect John Joseph Borie.*

In addition to its exhibition galleries on the top floor, Carpenter Hall contains in the library a large Renaissance mantelpiece from the Château of Chenonceaux, near Tours, brilliantly designed and bearing the initials and the salamander symbol of Francis I and Queen Claude. It makes an interesting comparison with the English example, of nearly a century later, at Amherst College.

From the Roman Empire, second to third century A.D., is an important sarcophagus panel, marble 19 by 47 inches, representing *Eros with Nereids, Tritons, and Seahorses.*[5] It was formerly in Wilton House, near Salisbury, the seat of the Earl of Pembroke. Finely chiseled and polished, it is filled with figures enacting themes with Eastern as well as classical connections. These are interestingly discussed in Octavio Alvarez, *The Celestial Brides: A Study in Mythology and Archaeology* (Stockbridge, Mass.: Herbert Reichner, 1978, number 143), where the Dartmouth relief is described as a Romanized version of the ancient and exotic love story between the soul and celestial females. Exceptional in reliefs of this kind is the intensity of the embrace of the female at the extreme left. The central Nereid approached by a Cupid bearing the wedding band appears on other sarcophagi; here her incipient captivation of the sea god is contested, or perhaps assisted, by a third female, who struggles with a rearing horse, another symbol of masculinity.

A flattening process, observable in the difference between the Williams College example of c. A.D. 300 and the Antioch mosaic of c. 500 at Worcester (MA 269 and MA 291), that effectively altered the style of late Roman mosaic is carried still further in Dartmouth's *Dog Ram-*

5

6

pant in Flying Gallop.[6] This panel is one of four fragments of a floor mosaic representing a hunt. It comes from Roman Syria, fifth to sixth century, and measures about 4 by 6 feet. Such scenes are closely related, in theme and design, to the art of neighboring Sassanian Persia. It is worth keeping in mind that the Justinian mosaics of Constantinople and Ravenna are little more than a century distant in the future, for Roman illusionism has all but completely disappeared here. A "carpet" effect now being desired, there is no longer a need for the minute tesserae that made such illusionism possible, nor for the wide range of colors that in Pompeiian times supported it. Nevertheless, the broad outlines manage to suggest rotundity, as does the circular arrangement of the tesserae themselves in the neck and chest areas of this alert animal.

Italian Renaissance painting is represented by an early *Madonna and Child with Saints Sebastian and Roch*,[7] by Marco Palmezzano (1459–c. 1545), who worked at Forli, across the Apennines northeast of Florence in the region known as Romagna. Painted in tempera on a panel 67 by 63 inches, it combines a Peruginesque quietude (see MA 250) with the somewhat dry manner that was in vogue in both Florence and Rome at the end of the fifteenth century. Distant connections with the Venetian art of Giovanni Bellini are also observable. Color is relatively subdued, but a lovely light suffuses the landscape background. The picture has suffered considerable damage. It dates from about 1490.

A Baroque oil representing *St. Paul Hermit and the Raven*, attributed to Giacinto Brandi (1621–91) has much of the dramatic force of the Currier Gallery's *Martyrdom of St. Bartholomew*, at Manchester (NH 23). It is fully discussed in an article in Dartmouth's well-illustrated publication, *Acquisitions, 1974–1978*.

A good color plate in the publication just cited records the startling beauty of Dartmouth's finest portrait, the *Governor John Wentworth*,[8] a pastel (now mounted on canvas) by John Singleton Copley (1738–

7

8

1815). Given to the college in 1977 by a collateral of the Wentworth family, it has been widely exhibited and published, notably in Jules Prown's definitive monograph on the painter (Cambridge: Harvard University Press, 1966). Smaller than Copley's "cabinet size" half-length oils, it nevertheless reaches a height of 2 feet. Copley's monogram and the date, 1769, appear at center right. Copley's forty known pastel portraits (as against the hundreds of oils he painted) were almost all executed prior to his departure for England in 1774, and there is none finer than his image of the last royal governor of New Hamphire. These pastels rival Europe's best, by Rosalba Carriera (1675–1757), Chardin (1699–1779), and Maurice Quentin de LaTour (1704–88). Such a feat is the more remarkable because Copley taught himself the technique, receiving some instruction only through correspondence with a talented Swiss practitioner of the medium who was living in London, Jean-Etienne Liotard (1702–89). The governor is shown at the age of thirty-two in a pale dove-gray silk coat flecked with rust red against the brown-gray tone of the background. His powdered hair strikes an exact balance between the tone of his coat and the whites about his neck. The ruddy flesh tones relate to the russet hues on his coat. The hair is presumably a wig, but Copley has made it appear to be a natural growth. Silvery, as in Gainsborough (see MA 306), is the word for the general effect—from hair to the silver buttons at the base of this masterpiece. Copley painted the governor in Portsmouth, then the provincial capital of New Hampshire. Many copies of the portrait were made by other painters, including one of 1878 in oils by Ulysses Dow Tenney that is owned by Dartmouth. Copley himself made a replica in pastel for John Hurd of Portsmouth—apparently commissioned because the original was about to be shipped to Paul Wentworth in London. A tradition that the beautiful frame was made by Paul Revere is unsubstantiated. (Further information will be found in articles in *Acquisitions, 1974–1978* and in *Portraits at Dartmouth*, by the curator, Arthur R. Blumenthal, 1978).

Like Thomas Cole, eight years his junior, Thomas Doughty (1793–1856) was a pioneer in the development of the Hudson River School of landscape painting. Dartmouth's *Rowing on a Mountain Lake*,[9] 17 by

9

44 inches, was painted about 1835. Its fine quality is such that it was included in "The Natural Paradise," an important exhibition staged in 1976 by the Museum of Modern Art that traced the continuity of American Romanticism in nature-painting from 1800 to 1950. Accompanying the illustration in the catalogue is a quotation from Ralph Waldo Emerson (1836): "The world proceeds from the same spirit as the body of man. It is a remoter and inferior incarnation of God, a projection of God in the unconscious. But it differs from the body in one important respect. It is not, like that, now subjected to the human will. Its serene order is inviolable to us." Born in Philadelphia and self-trained, Doughty settled in New York in 1838 following a brief trip to England. In New York he died, impoverished and little appreciated, though he had had considerable success in his most productive years. In *Painting in America* (New York: Crowell, 1956, page 157), E. P. Richardson suggests that a comparable Doughty of 1835 in Detroit "has something of the quality of Bryant's poem, *To a Waterfowl*, and Doughty, like Bryant, was one of the first to see this wild and lonely continent as a theme for art."

A brilliant small oil on panel by William Merritt Chase (1849–1916), undated, bears the title *The Lone Fisherman*,[10] but it conveys no such awesome solitude or hermetic darkness as marks Doughty's image of perhaps seventy-five years earlier. A stout seawall backed by piled-up rocks leads us violently on a diagonal—perhaps suggested by compositions of Degas—to the fisherman, who seems much more actively engaged than Doughty's prisoner of nature primeval. The sea is a dazzling blue. Such intensity is unusual in Chase's work; and his landscapes are generally much more placid. If you will turn the illustration upside down, you will discover how powerful is the play of diagonals in this picture. Technically, Chase was a virtuoso who managed in his later years to combine the high-intensity palette of the French Impressionists with the spirited brushwork of John Singer Sargent. He spent five years in study abroad, including nine months in Venice with the American Frank Duveneck. Returning in 1878, as E. P. Richardson says, "with a halo of European success," he opened a studio on West Tenth Street in

10

New York and also taught at the newly organized Art Students League. As a teacher, he was enormously influential. When John W. Twachtman died in 1902, Chase took his place in a group of New York and Boston painters who first exhibited in 1898 in New York under the name of Ten American Painters. Including such masters as Frank W. Benson (see MA 168) and Childe Hassam (see MA 182), they formed, in Richardson's words, "a kind of academy of American Impressionism."

It is no great leap in time, but light-years in the development of modern art, to turn from Chase to *Guitar on a Table*[11] by Pablo Picasso (1881–1973). An oil 2 feet high painted in 1912/13, it is some five years later than Boston's *Standing Figure* (MA 87) and about six years before *La Table*, owned by Smith College (MA 185). Between 1908 and 1920, in close association with Georges Braque, Picasso developed Cubism to its nearly monochromatic gray-and-tan stage and then gradually reintroduced color into the century's most important visual invention. The Dartmouth picture, once owned by Gertrude Stein and later by Nelson A. Rockefeller (a Dartmouth graduate), is a superb example of the early return of color to Cubist painting. It is not strictly an "oil" because Picasso first drew the major lines in charcoal and introduced sand into the oil medium for textural effect. As of 1911 he began to work in collage (pasted papers), partly for their texture and chiefly as a means of achieving a playful dichotomy between reality and illusion. The papers, usually printed newspapers, patterned oilcloth, or simulated wood grain, are "real" but their reality is clearly at best only incidental to the picture's content; it is therefore illusory. What is real is the illusion of objects disassembled and reconstructed according to the painter's imagination. Quickly following on the first collages, the idea came to Picasso to paint illusions of them, to achieve, as it were, his own complete reality. Paintings of this period are much flatter than those of tan-and-gray Cubism of 1910/11, and they look like assemblages of papers laid onto the picture surface. The Dartmouth example is finely composed with its activity revolving around its black center. Pale ochers, greens, and blues gently enliven the varied near-whites. The guitar has been taken apart and its basic shapes rearranged to form the design. For a true collage of the same period, but still lingering in Picasso's gray-and-tan tonal limits, see *Glasses and Newspaper* by his younger compatriot and protégé, Juan Gris (MA 184).

From the series of frescoes by José Clemente Orozco (1883–1949) in the Baker Library, one called *The Departure of Quetzalcoatl* is illustrated here.[12] Orozco spent two rather frenetic years (1932–34) on this

11

12

important commission: such tension is hardly surprising when a highly temperamental artist is set in a traditional center of learning. Although the murals are certainly not conducive to the sense of restfulness and quiet essential to a study area, the visitor should know that Orozco did not select the location for his frescoes and was by no means happy about it. Nevertheless, the series as a whole ranks among the best works of Mexico's most gifted painter. As such, it contributes significantly to the cultural life of the college. Moreover, one should not forget, any more than medieval monks did in their time, the importance of owning an object of pilgrimage. Dartmouth is increasingly discovering its debt to those intrepid souls who brought Orozco to Hanover. The frescoes seem to some extent the victim of their own propaganda, but they serve as a reminder of cultures other than our own; and since they commemorate the overthrow of oppression in Mexico we may be reminded, however obliquely, of our own Revolution. Measuring 10 by 17 feet, *The Departure of Quetzalcoatl* is one of the largest of the frescoes. As legendary god and Toltec ruler, Quetzalcoatl stands for the forces of light and goodness in their combat with darkness and evil. To him is ascribed the discovery of maize, the arts, science, and the calendar.

In approaching the art of Jean Dubuffet (born 1901) we should clarify the meaning of *l'art brut*, with which he is closely associated. Such art is indeed brutal at times, but the word means rough or unrefined, as in rough-cut diamond or *champagne brut*. In an important exhibition held in 1961 at the Museum of Modern Art, "The Art of Assemblage," the title came from a word championed by Dubuffet himself. He felt that *collage* should be reserved for "collages made in the period 1910–1920 by the Dadaists, Picasso and Braque, etc." For some years Dubuffet had extended the original idea of collage to all manner of unexpected materials and into three dimensions as well. "I have always loved—it is a sort of vice—to employ only the most common materials in my work, those that one does not dream of at first because they are too crude and close at hand and seem unsuitable for anything whatsoever. I like to proclaim that my art is an enterprise to rehabilitate discredited values."

In an age without heroes such an artistic program is surely relevant. Well trained in the academies of Paris, Dubuffet quickly challenged their axioms and assumptions, collected and exhibited the art of the insane, explored graffiti scratched on urban walls, promulgated the art of children, loaded his canvases with soot, debris, and cut-up scraps— and in general exploited his belief that art should be "stripped of all the tinsel, laurels and buskins in which it has been decked, and be seen naked with all the creases of its belly."

Dartmouth's *Topographie au Nid de Pierres*,[13] an assemblage of 1958 on a canvas measuring 3 by 5 feet, belongs to a series made from various paintings of basic elements composing the earth's surface; these were then cut up and the pieces newly juxtaposed. His project was "the execution of a cycle of large paintings celebrating the ground." The title of the Dartmouth picture is essentially untranslatable, but we may venture a paraphrase to the effect that this is an impression (but in no sense a description) of bare rocky ground seen from above. In his comment on these paintings in the catalogue of the Museum of Modern Art's Dubuffet retrospective of 1962, the artist wrote of being captivated by the "opportunity afforded of composing paintings by the simple method of juxtaposing textures on which there were no objects with clearly defined contours."

Our last selection, a construction of iron, steel, and wood measuring 11 by 18 by 10 feet and entitled *X-Delta*,[14] was acquired in 1976 and erected on the lawn of the Baker Library. A brief look at our first selection, the ancient Roman marble relief, will indicate dramatically the long road that sculpture has traveled; it will also help explain why not all the citizenry of Hanover approve of this enormous interloper. The history of the Orozco frescoes, however, suggests that time will heal all wounds. The artist of this piece is Mark di Suvero, born 1933 and in New York circles considered the leading monumental sculptor of his generation. *X-Delta* was the sensation of the Whitney Museum's Annual in 1970, the year of its execution. In the tradition of David Smith (see MA 88), but much closer to modern skyscraper and bridge construction, and in some ways suggestive of the paintings of Franz Kline (see MA 279), it stretches its powerful diagonals, while a free-swinging metal platform introduces actual movement whenever it is pushed.

Our survey of Dartmouth's important collection has had to omit many fine works. Artists we should have liked to discuss include Alma-Tadema (see MA 258), Thomas Eakins (MA 17), John Sloan (ME 17), Fernand Léger (CT 84), Fritz Glarner, and especially Mark Rothko. Dartmouth's Rothko, an oil of 1953 nearly 10 feet high, is accurately described by its title, *Orange and Lilac over Ivory*. The values are so close, however, that a photograph would show only meaningless grays. It is one of the very fine works of the artist (1903–70), whose influence has been as profound as the magic of his veils of color.

The collection of modern art at Dartmouth, with generous representation in all media, and extending from Cubism to the present, makes it one of New England's five or six leading centers in this field.

13

14

The Currier Gallery of Art

Location: 192 Orange Street
Hours: Tues.-Sat. 10-4, Sun. 2-5; closed national holidays
Admission: Free. Ⓗ

This fine museum opened to the public in 1929. It was built in memory of Moody Currier, a governor of the state of New Hampshire, on the site of the Currier mansion in pleasantly landscaped grounds. Under a series of discriminating directors and wise trustees, it has become one of the leading small museums of New England. The most important acquisitions are published in a bulletin, and a well-illustrated handbook (including some thirty excellent color plates, but with no descriptive text) was published in 1979.

Also celebrating its fiftieth anniversary, the gallery inaugurated a building campaign that will provide balancing wings at the rear of the original structure. This welcome addition of space for exhibitions and services should be completed about the time of the appearance of the present book.

Apart from its paintings and sculptures, the gallery offers fine displays of decorative arts, principally American, with emphasis on furniture of New Hampshire origin. Some of New England's leading silversmiths are also represented, notably John Coney (1652–1722) of Boston, in one of his best designs, a sugar box of the 1690s.

Two items of particular local interest are *Amoskeag Canal*,[15] painted in Manchester in 1948 by Charles Sheeler (1883–1965) on commission from the gallery, and the *Merino Ram Weather Vane* of c. 1855, possibly made in the metalwork shops of the Amoskeag Manufacturing Company. While Sheeler's image of Manchester's factories, celebrated for their architectural purity, is not quite so "immaculate" as his *Upper Deck*, discussed at the Fogg Art Museum (MA 132), there is a kind of

15

16

Roger Sherman Spartanism (CT 75) about this industrial scene. Yet it is more complex than it at first appears. The varieties of red and pink are subtle, as are the variations on that endlessly repeated shape, the rectangle. The most important of these, the rise in window height at the left, occurs in the building itself, but we can easily imagine that Sheeler would have invented it if it had not existed.

The *Ram Weather Vane*, with its lightning rod, is one of the largest of its kind (73 inches wide and 11 inches across the body), and one of the finest in design. According to tradition it came from a mid-nineteenth century woolen mill, and it is worth noting that the Merino strain of sheep was early introduced into America to improve the quality of the wool. The ram is made of two layers of welded sheet copper, and there are traces of the gold leaf that once covered it. In profile, note how the curve of the horns finds echoing ripples and droops along the underside. Not to be missed, however, is the broad-beamed frontal view, with its impression of great strength. Like so many of the Early American limners, designers of weather vanes remain anonymous.

From a pair of superb portraits, subjects unknown, by William Jennys (active 1795–1805), we have selected the *Portrait of a Woman* for illustration. Comparison with the *Reuben Hatch* at New London (CT 87), signed and dated 1802, will quickly indicate that the unsigned Manchester portraits are by the same hand. They can be safely dated in approximately the same year. Fetchingly ugly in her pink dress, with face tones of pink and much gray, this woman has the harsh but native dignity seen in Walker Evans's photographs of the Depression years. Her husband, likewise popping into view in his oval inner frame, is perhaps more conventionally portrayed, but his stringy hair is yet another instance of the uncompromising honesty of this gifted American painter.

As impressive as it is rare outside Italian museums and churches is an anonymous Tuscan painting of the *Madonna and Child*,[18] in tempera on

18

17

panel measuring 37 by 20 inches. Its date, c. 1275, places it near the time of the birth of Giotto (see MA 33) and some fifty years before Simone Martini's altarpiece at the Gardner Museum in Boston (MA 34). Its formula is wholly Byzantine, but a Florentine inflection already appears in the squatter proportions and in the relative emphasis on physical bulk. The scarlet mantle projects brilliantly from the surrounding greenish gray of the robe and coif. Originally the curtain behind the throne was dark green, while the upper background and the frame were coated with silver foil. The frame was rectangular, not semicircular as now: an original section remains above the Virgins's head. This image may be called half icon, half relief sculpture in its total effect. Already Tuscan art is moving in the direction of Giotto. On the basis of its style, the picture has been attributed to the Florentine master Meliore, or to his circle.

At the head of the main staircase hangs a magnificent *Gothic tapestry*[19] woven at Tournai about 1490. This is a well-known example, often illustrated in books on tapestry making. As was usually the case, it formed part of a series for the decoration of a large hall. Others in the series have been preserved, two of them in the Corcoran Gallery, Washington, D.C. The scene is generally identified as *The Visit of the Gypsies.* Arriving at the left, they are met by the lord and lady of the castle, but it is not at all certain that they will be admitted. A hunt is in progress high up in the background. The escutcheon at the top was added about 1600 by a new owner. The Gothic tapestry makers characteristically limited themselves to about thirty different wools, with the result that the colors, in which reds and blues predominate, stand out well at a distance. Similar results were obtained in medieval stained glass. Because the designers had no thought of natural illusion, they were free to make the decoration of a wall an occasion for creating an enchanted world. Sacheverell Sitwell chose this tapestry as his point of departure in writing "The Gothick North."

To what extent the North felt the influence of the Italian Renaissance may be seen in a comparison of Manchester's *Self-Portrait*[20] by Jan Gossaert, called Mabuse (c. 1478–1532), with the *Portrait of a Lady*[21]

19

20

by Lorenzo Costa of Ferrara (1460–1535). Both are about 18 inches high, and both were painted in oil on panel, although the Costa has been transferred to canvas (a difficult operation necessitated by warping and cracking of the original panel). The more squarish shape of the Italian picture (18 by 14 inches as against 17 by 12 for the Gossaert) corresponds to Italian-classical traditions as against Gothic verticality, as also seen in the architecture of the two regions.

Gossaert, whom we shall see again at Providence in an ambitious drawing of *Adam and Eve* (RI 10), started his career at Antwerp, but a trip to Italy about 1508 turned him from inherited Flemish forms toward uniting them with Italian ones. Identified as a self-portrait by two authorities independently, it can be dated around 1518–20. The eyes look as if into a mirror, while the right hand (assuming this is a mirror image) is hidden to disguise the fact that it is engaged with the pencil or brush. We can admire the skill of Gossaert's mannered Italianate nudes (RI 10), but only in his portraits do we sense that he was free from a desire to show off. Face and hand are equally expressive, and the several blacks contrast superbly with the red hat and the bright green ground.

Lorenzo Costa, after painting in Ferrara and Bologna, had the good fortune to be called to Mantua in 1506 by that great patroness of the arts, Duchess Isabella d'Este. He remained there until his death in 1535. The Currier's portrait was formerly thought to represent Eleonora Gonzaga, of the ruling family at Mantua, but in 1978 the gallery's *Bulletin* published a long study by John E. Schloder that demonstrated the error of such an identification, and through an elaborate study of Costa's known work set the date of the picture back from c. 1506, as previously believed, to c. 1497. Whoever the lady may be, she is shown against a black ground in a green dress with a red bodice and sleeves of brownish-red and yellow. Against this mass of hard color her delicate skin contrasts with stylish pallor. To keep it so, the artist has held the shadows to a minimum; he has achieved the desired sculptural effect through a web of thin lines (bodice, necklaces, headdress, wisps of

21

hair). It is worth looking closely to see how Costa has made them push inward and outward to model the form.

Compared with the Gossaert portrait, this Renaissance image is characteristically big in scale, solidly planted on its invisible base, aggressively modeled, and serenely confident, whereas Gossaert seems to look at himself through the eyes of one of Jan van Eyck's pious donors.

The *Madonna and Child* by Pietro Perugino (1445–1523) can match neither the expressiveness nor the strength of modeling of the *Sepulcrum Christi*, discussed at the Clark Art Institute (MA 250); but its authentication as a work of the master by a long list of experts would be difficult to refute. That it was long ago proclaimed to be the work of Raphael, however, may be taken to demonstrate the advance of modern connoisseurship. The picture has a distinguished provenance, almost back to the time of its execution, around 1500, and to the famed collection of Agostino Chigi for his Villa Farnesina in Rome. Truth to say, it is fully characteristic of Perugino's flaccid art; and thus it offers yet another reason to wonder how Perugino could have been totally responsible for the marvelous picture in Williamstown.

The *Holy Family*[22] by Joos van Cleve (1485–1540), born in the lower Rhenish town of his name but, like his contemporary Jan Gossaert, active in Antwerp, illustrates once again a Northerner's attempt to graft Italian humanism onto inherited traditions. Renaissance effects are found in the soft flesh modeling and in the Italianate column. Flemish elements remain in the precise detail, in Joseph's wooden pose (and his straw hat), in the foreground still life and the landscape background, in the Gothic hand of Joseph's scroll, and in the carved Gothic paneling below it. A similar composition is owned by the Metropolitan Museum of Art, New York. The suggested date of c. 1520–25 places the Currier's picture as almost exactly contemporary with Jan Gossaert's *Self-Portrait*.

By the seventeenth century, Italian painting was in full Baroque sway. In the *Martyrdom of St. Bartholomew*[23] by Mattia Preti (1613–69) the Currier Gallery has a potent example. A canvas over 6 feet square, it

22

23

dates from c. 1655–60. The head of the bearded old Saint has much in common with Bernini's clay head of *St. Jerome* at the Fogg Art Museum (MA 121), of approximately the same period. Born in Calabria, Preti studied in Rome under the strong influence of the followers of Caravaggio (see CT 12), and worked primarily in Naples. The Manchester painting was part of a triptych—probably the central element—which also represented the martyrdoms of Saints Peter and Paul. The massive figure of Bartholomew, his eyes turned to heaven, is dramatically spotlighted while his torturers go about their terrible work in half darkness. The Saint's right arm has already been flayed. As we have suggested in other instances, the power of the design—its clashing diagonals and its tight clusters of figures at the extremities—will come through with great force if the illustration is turned upside down. (It does so right side up, but you can easily overlook it as you explore the formidable interest of the details.) In the proper position note the power of the three heads at the lower right, one jutting forward, one erect, the third turned away. Of such "push-and-pull" combinations—to borrow a phrase from the modern abstractionist Hans Hofmann—Baroque art produces its explosive energy. It also exploits textural contrasts, as here in the opaque highlights as against the thinly applied darks that allow the grain of the canvas to show through. Seen against a cold greenish-blue sky of low intensity, the Baroque drama reaches a pitch seldom matched in seventeenth-century paintings in American museums.

That the spirit of the Baroque was not limited to martyrdoms, or to Italy, will quickly be discovered in a superb Dutch landscape, *View of Egmond-on-the-Sea*,[24] signed and dated 1648 by Jacob van Ruisdael (1628/9–82). A smallish (26 by 20 inches) oil on panel painted when the artist was only twenty years old, it prefigures his masterly marine at Boston (MA 74) by two decades. It is so highly regarded that in 1954 the Metropolitan Museum of Art included it in a memorable exhibition of "Dutch Painting in the Golden Age," the greater part of which was lent from major European collections. Among painters prior to Ruisdael, landscape was almost always conceived as the background to something else; in the century after him it fought a losing battle against the con-

24

ventions of the Rococo park, the classical ruin, or the storm-racked coast. *View of Egmond* is landscape as pure as those of Constable and Monet in the nineteenth century. Yet it is still touched by the medieval sense of wonder, in the artificially darkened foreground with its strange formations and shadowy figures—and the unforgettable tree. How it swirls around its axis, propelling us along the picture's serpentine course deep into the distance! Baroque? Indeed it is; in the disguise of nature this wildly contorted trunk is nothing less than a twisted column from Bernini's bronze *baldacchino* under the dome of St. Peter's.

Much of this spirit lingers in *The Storm*,[25] painted in 1759 by Claude-Joseph Vernet (1714–89). For all its headlong rush, however, the action seems more restricted to the surface than Ruisdael's movement of powerful masses into space. An early exponent of what was to become nineteenth-century Romanticism, Vernet was inspired more by the *idea* of nature untamed than by creative imagination. The canvas is choked with awe-provoking clichés of disaster: ships leaning at dangerous angles, a blasted tree (à la Salvator Rosa), a grim castle surmounting a lonely rock, lashing waves, gesticulating people, an expiring victim. A single hole of blue pokes through the leaden skies. What is lacking here is the *painter's* equivalent of James Thomson's apostrophe to Winter in his poem of 1726 ("Cogenial horrors, hail!"), or of the storm in the third movement of Beethoven's Sixth Symphony. Discussing a very different work by Vernet in the Louvre (*The Ponte Rotto, Rome*)—one that magically links Claude Lorrain with Camille Corot—Paul Jamot wrote that it shows "what he was capable of, had he been able to resist the dictates of fashion" (*La Peinture en France*; Paris: Plon, 1934).

As for Corot himself (1796–1875), the Currier owns a small masterpiece, *Grez-sur-Loing: Bridge and Church*[26] of the 1850s, slightly later than Yale's limpid *La Rochelle* (CT 78) and a quarter-century after Smith College's crystalline *Jumièges* (MA 177). Situated just south of

25

26

the forest of Fontainebleau, Grez attracted many painters of the Barbizon School. Since Corot was one of the primary sources for the art of Claude Monet (1840–1926) and the Currier also owns a major early work by this leading Impressionist, *The Seine at Bougival*,[27] a comparison is appropriate. Despite the long interval between the births of the two artists, the pictures are not far removed in time: the Corot is fairly late and the Monet was probably painted in 1869 in the outlying Parisian village frequented that year and later by Renoir (see MA 83). In both paintings the space is fenced off by a series of small elements parallel to the picture surface. Monet works in a deeper space, but Corot is at pains to emphasize the bridge and the church. Monet is dazzled by his new discovery of light and fresh color, to which the oil and watercolor sketches of Constable may have contributed. The apple greens, rust reds, oranges, and pale blues shine out from this world of slate and buff; and Monet is on the verge of moving into the full Impressionism of the "rainbow palette." It is possible to admire this stage of his art more than the later realization; the point is mentioned because Monet's early work is too easily passed off as a step toward something else. If he had died in 1870, he would still rank as a master of consequence.

Corot worked at a lower emotional pitch, and his color intensities are appropriately muted. Through his subtle "feathery" screen we are led to his well-modeled architectural masses. The strongest light establishes the not-quite-exact center of his composition. How dull a series of arches parading left to right might have been! But Corot makes each one different, profits by the break left of center, and like the Little Dutch masters he so admired discovers all manner of detail to enliven this long link between the two extremes of his picture.

Before we move into the twentieth century, a listing of paintings omitted with regret, and only because of restrictions of space, is inserted here. For the seventeenth century, the large *Banquet of Anthony and Cleopatra* by Jan de Bray of Haarlem, possibly alluding to the artist's own marriage in the year he painted this picture; and a superb *Still Life* of c. 1650 by an unknown Spanish artist more delicate and precise than his formidable predecessor, van der Hamen y León (see MA 274). For

27

the eighteenth century, *The First Lessons in Love* by Jean-Baptiste Greuze, in which a miracle of painting overcomes the pettiness of its theme. For the early nineteenth century, the *Portrait of a Musician* by Pauline Auzou (1809), almost comparable to the work of Jacques Louis David (see MA 125), whose strong influence she felt; and John Constable's *Dedham Mill* (c. 1820), a bit smoother than usual, but already rich in the greens that helped liberate French landscape painting from the domination of Old Master browns. For American nineteenth-century landscape, excellent examples by Bierstadt, Birch, Cropsey, and a Heade (*Marshfield Meadows*) that rivals the one discussed at Bowdoin College (ME 14).

There are several fine American paintings from the first quarter of the twentieth century. Leading the list is a late portrait by Thomas Eakins, *Miss Florence Einstein* (1905, one year after Smith College's *Mrs. Edith Mahon*, MA 176). Robert Henri's *Girl*, c. 1910, is even more characteristic than Mount Holyoke's example (MA 207); Charles Demuth's watercolor of rooftops close to Williams's *Trees and Barns* of 1917 (MA 276); and Edward Hopper's *Bootleggers* of 1924 not yet in the full stride of Andover's *Manhattan Bridge Loop* (MA 20).

One would not ordinarily think of Walt Kuhn (see ME 42) and Georges Rouault together, but they were both born in the 1870s and the Currier's fine examples date from 1939 and represent circus people. *Lancer*, a healthy American girl, rather like a drum majorette dressed in red, white, and blue, contrasts strikingly with Rouault's *Wounded Clown*,[28] an unusually large oil-on-paper-on-Masonite measuring 6 by 4 feet. As so often happens in such comparisons, we see a brash new world juxtaposed with an introverted, complex old one. Both painters load the brush heavily, but it is Rouault who lingers over his strokes, introducing subtle variations within a color area, and so manipulating the textures as to provide a wonderful sense of light shining through from behind. Kuhn portrays his subject objectively, as he saw her; Rouault's three figures are somehow symbolic of the human condition. The ambiguity of his title is appropriate. Which clown is wounded? The old one, seated at the left as if exhausted? The young clown and/or

28

his companion, sadly preoccupied with the book they hold? We do not require an answer. Blacks play a major role among the dominant reds and blues of this picture. Heavily outlining the rich color areas, they help create the illusion that we are looking at a Gothic stained-glass window. They also model volumes: stomachs, knees, thighs. Behind the head of the old clown they hollow out an ominous cave.

Twenty years ago, to come upon Picasso's *Woman Seated in a Chair*,[29] a 51-by-38-inch composition of 1941, was an astonishing experience in the generally conservative atmosphere of this museum. Much has happened since to give it company, but still its *modernity* is here unsurpassed. We should perhaps point out that it was not a purchase but a gift in 1951, and an anonymous one. If the community has not wholly taken the lady to its heart, she at least serves as a reminder that time marches on. Picasso's precarious vertical constructions and the importance of the dagger shapes in his disquieting art for a disquieting era have been pointed out (see MA 185). Here the full range of color that we might find in the Alhambra is called into play, together with its superposition of patterns. The composition was influenced by Matisse in the big curves of the chair, binding together all these stacked angles. We hesitate to call this chair a Windsor, and we should never call this personage a Woman. The painting is an object in its own right, flat yet spacious, abstract yet sinister, gaudy yet harmonious; an optical jam session if you will, but featuring a star performer.

Another *Seated Woman*,[30] this time nude and with arms clasped behind her head, brings us to sculpture and to Picasso's chief rival in modernity, Henri Matisse (1869–1954). For evidence of modernity, contrast this bronze with Augustus Saint-Gaudens's lovely *Diana* of 1893 (NH 3), of which the Currier owns a small bronze replica. Purchased in 1964, the Matisse figure was completed in 1925 and cast in an edition of ten. In profile it exists in an imaginary square some 32 inches on a side; but it should be seen from many angles, for it is over a foot broad and the transitions as you walk around it are subtle indeed. Its vitality is extraordinary, emerging in part from the risky balance of the pose, in part from the powerful jut of the elbows and the raised

29

30

left knee, and perhaps most of all from the harsh shift of planes in the modeling itself. Such modeling relates directly to Matisse's painting, especially in the mid-1920s following a relaxed period of soft, rather indolent odalisques. It marked a return to his normally vigorous style, influenced from the start by the painting of Paul Cézanne.

In his ambitious monumental creations the modernism of Sir Jacob Epstein (1880–1959), New York–born but working in England from the age of twenty-five, is gross and now sadly dated. But as a portraitist Epstein was one of the leading figures of his generation. He intensified the realism of Rodin (see MA 308), giving it an almost Etruscan effect of actuality. *Portrait of Kitty*,[31] the third version of a likeness of his daughter, was modeled in 1957. Its green patina is especially effective in catching the light on its churned surfaces. The deeply hollowed pupils give strong focus to the gaze, as does the tousled bobbed hair. We are made very conscious that this head was conceived and executed in clay; and the superb casting does not betray that origin. As such, the precariousness of the head's support on a very thin neck and very narrow shoulders is all the more remarkable and expressive. Through kinetic means a feeling of empathy is somehow enlisted.

The American sculptor Dimitri Hadzi, born in New York in 1921, gained international acceptance during the 1960s. *Floating Helmets*, a major bronze of 1965, has a prominent position in the sculpture garden of the Yale University Art Gallery (a smaller study for it is owned by Mount Holyoke College). In 1978 the Currier purchased *Hephaestus III*,[32] a bronze of 1971/2, 6 feet tall, the second cast of an edition of seven. Unlike Epstein's *Kitty III*, this piece was designed for its ultimate realization in metal—and very heavy metal indeed. The great double-ax shapes, though irregular, evoke memories of ancient Crete. If Hephaestus (the Roman Vulcan) frequented Mt. Olympus rather than Mt. Ida, and the volcanic islands of the Aegean Sea and Sicily rather than Crete itself, we shall not quarrel, for the forms are most appropriate to the god of fire and metalwork. Their power is portentous; such images can suggest

31

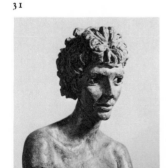

32

destruction. Too many people, hurrying into Avery Fisher Hall at Lincoln Center to hear the New York Philharmonic, have not noticed in the lobby Hadzi's *K. 458 The Hunt*, inspired by a Mozart quartet.

In our survey of paintings in the Currier Gallery we ended on the theme of modernity with Picasso's *Woman Seated in a Chair*. But that work dates from 1941; in the interim modernity has spawned new forms in painting as in sculpture. In the past few years, the gallery has been active in filling in the gap with admirable purchases of paintings by such artists as Olitzki, Anuszkiewicz, Albers, and Gottlieb. Adolf Gottlieb (1903–73) was a leading member of the so-called New York Abstract Expressionists. His 6-by-8-foot canvas, painted in 1956, bears the title *From Midnight to Dawn*.[33] As always in such art, we should resist the temptation to "read" the painting from associations suggested by its title —which was almost certainly an afterthought. (The alternative would have been *Number X, 1956*, but Gottlieb preferred more specific identifications.) His canvas is a huge, dark blue field, varied in texture like a Mark Rothko, with light seeming to shine through from behind, and boldly marked with strokes of deep black. Activity sputters across the top—in a frieze suspended over the void.

33

Vermont

Vermont

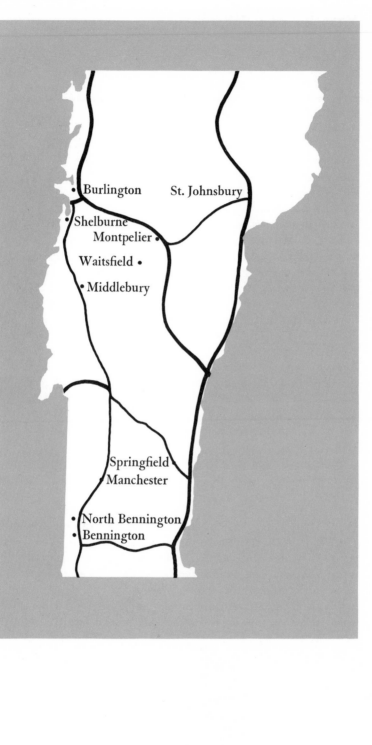

Bennington Museum

Location: West Main St. (Vermont Route 9), 1 mile west of Route 9 inter-
section with U.S. 7
Telephone: (802) 442-2180
Hours: 9-5 daily, including Sun. and holidays; but closed December, January,
and February, and on Thanksgiving Day
Admission: Charged. Ⓗ but phone ahead

Primarily a museum of southwestern Vermont history, with a supporting
research library, this well-appointed building also serves as an art
museum. It contains mementos of the Battle of Bennington (1777),
an array of U.S. flags (including the oldest one in existence, now so
faded as paradoxically to resemble a modern Jasper Johns version in
gray oils), military collections, costumes, the largest collection anywhere
of ceramics made in Bennington, a superbly shown and very extensive
display of American glass, fine furniture, household items, and dolls
and toys.

Early American paintings include Ralph Earl's *Portrait of Captain
Elijah Dewey*, commander of the Bennington militia at the Battle of
Bennington (his house, now the nearby Walloomsac Inn, appears in the
distance); William Jenny's *Portraits of Governor Paul Brigham and
His Wife* (comparable in quality to CT 87 and NH 17); and several
oils by William Morris Hunt (unfortunately skied and in need of
cleaning).

An especially good weather vane featuring horse and driver came
from the Putnam barn in the vicinity. Outstanding among the sculptures,
however, are two animal groups by Antoine Louis Barye (1796–1875)
and a small bronze by Auguste Rodin (1840–1917). *Leopard with
Prey*,[1] about 3 feet long and the larger of the Barye bronzes, was
modeled in 1850. This version was exhibited at the Paris World's Fair
in 1889. While many New England museums represent this major
sculptor in small bronzes, few can show him at a scale that does full
justice to his power. It is a commonplace to call him the alter ego in
sculpture of Eugène Delacroix (1798–1863); but it would be equally
appropriate to reverse the two names. Comparison with MA 120 will

1

indicate the connection. Exact contemporaries and lifelong friends, they studied wild animals together in the Paris zoo (better known as the Jardin des Plantes). The strength of the leopard in this superb design finds expression in Baroque forms whose source leads back to Bernini and the seventeenth century. Traces of gilding persist in this piece, but its true "color" comes from its carefully marked surfaces, modeled as only a sculptor knows how to model them, and then drawn upon.

The little Rodin bronze, only a foot high, is a greenish patinated cast of a plaster in the Musée Rodin in Paris, there listed as *Petite Ombre, Numéro 1* and dated 1888. A second "Small Shade," strained and emaciated like the first, likewise found its place in the sculptor's vast project for the *Gates of Hell*, inspired by Dante's *Inferno*. (For another work connected with this project, see MA 308, a head that, reworked, became a portrait of Eleanora Duse but is known as *Sorrow.* That title, while also appropriate for the Bennington figure, has the disadvantage of causing confusion.) Bennington's *Petite Ombre* is deeply expressive from all points of view, and like the *Leopard* bronze of Barye, by whom Rodin was profoundly influenced, it should be exhibited free-standing in order to allow such inspection. As for this particular bronze cast, which bears the stamp of the great Rudier foundry, it is difficult to tell when it was made. Casts of Rodin's plasters were produced in his lifetime and frequently after his death; the posthumous ones did not always record the ultimate subtleties of the original.

Sculpture of a very different kind appears in a 10-foot *Monumental Piece* created by Christopher Fenton's U.S. Pottery Company of Bennington for the 1853 Crystal Palace Exposition in New York. It incorporates most of the known processes for which Bennington ceramics became celebrated. The Madonna at the summit and the bust of Fenton are of unglazed white Parian ware; pedestals and pillars are of multicolored glazed flint enamel; the molded columns lower down are in the mottled brown glaze properly called Rockingham rather than Bennington; and the bottom section is of scrodded ware worked to resemble veined marble. Aesthetically this creation leaves something to be desired, but it is perhaps captious to say so.

A carved and gilded wooden *Eagle* of 1795, nobly impressive, will not be overlooked by the visitor; but a painted *British Drum* of 1757 could well escape the attention. This object was captured at the Battle of Bennington; its figured circumference is not uninteresting.

An extra attraction here is the gallery of paintings by "Grandma Moses" (Anna Mary Robertson, 1860–1961), who took up painting in the early 1900s, but did not make a career of it until 1938, at the age of seventy-eight. In her remaining twenty-three years she produced some fifteen hundred pictures. In 1972 the old schoolhouse that she had attended more than a century before was moved from nearby Eagle Bridge, N.Y., to form a separate extension of the Bennington Museum. It had been fitted out as the Grandma Moses Schoolhouse Museum by the artist's son, Forrest Moses, and his wife. The memorabilia include the stained-glass window of the W. D. Thomas pharmacy in Hoosick Falls, N.Y., where she sold her first paintings (at three dollars and five dollars, depending on the size). Since she lived in Bennington for eight years, from 1927 to 1935, it is fitting that her memorial should be here. She died nationally honored, and particularly acclaimed by another amateur artist, Dwight D. Eisenhower.

Visitors to the museum should not fail to visit the nearby First Congregational Church, a gem of the Federal Style built in 1806 by Lavius Fillmore, and its graveyard with excellent examples of the stonecutter's craft.

In the fall of 1981, announcement was made of the acquisition of Ralph Earl's important, large, and very fine *Landscape of Bennington*, painted in 1798. The gambrel-roofed house of Capt. Elijah Dewey, whose portrait is mentioned above, appears again in the landscape view of the original town. Earl's portrait of Mrs. Elijah Dewey will also be added to the collection.

Bennington College

Location: From Route 7 north of Bennington, exit west on Route 67A and follow to the entrance to the campus, on the right
Hours: Daily except from mid-December to mid-March, when the college is not in session
Admission: Free

An important center for the study and practice of contemporary modern art, Bennington College has resisted a policy of forming a permanent collection. Through the years it has attracted leading figures as instructors, and its alumnae (and now alumni)—including Helen Frankenthaler (see MA 222)—have made their mark. The Usdan Gallery, located off the entrance to the college's vast Visual and Performing Arts Center, offers frequently changing exhibitions, primarily of the work of artists in New York City. Scattered about the grounds and in various college buildings, however, the visitor may come upon work by such sculptors as David Smith, Anthony Caro, and Isaac Witkin, and paintings by Helen Frankenthaler, Pat Adams, Paul Feeley, Kenneth Noland, and Jules Olitski.

The college owns a bronze *Portrait Bust of John Dewey* by Sir Jacob Epstein (see NH 31), one of two such casts of a clay original of 1927. The other was purchased by Dewey's students at Columbia University and presented to Teachers College. As the guiding spirit of progressive education, Dewey became a kind of father figure for Bennington College at the time of its opening in 1932. Of his bust, Epstein has written, "Dewey's son-in-law said . . . that I had made him look like a 'Vermont horse dealer.' This was not a bad characterization, as Professor Dewey came from Vermont; and he pleased me with his Yankee drawl and seeming casualness. He was a man absolutely straightforward, simple, and lovable in character. Professor Dewey said of his bust that it pleased him and he 'hoped he looked like it' " (*Let There Be Sculpture*; New York: Putnam, 1940).

The Park-McCullough House

Location: Park St., near the center of town; from Route 7 north of Bennington exit west on Route 67A
Hours: May 1-October 31, Mon.-Fri. 10-4, Sun. 12-4
Admission: Charged. Ⓗ projected

For a description of this great house, built in 1865 of white clapboards over brick and containing thirty-two rooms in its high-ceilinged three stories, see the companion volume in this series, *A Guide to Historic Houses of New England*, by Margaret Supplee Smith. On the lawn, do not miss the dollhouse replica of the cupola atop this imposing pile.

A hundred years after its construction, the house was opened as a museum and has developed into an active cultural center in the community. The elaborate furnishings are notable, and they include paintings by Kensett and Bierstadt of the Hudson River School.

Robert Hull Fleming Museum, University of Vermont

Location: Colchester Ave. Take exit 14W off I-89; from Williston Rd. turn left onto East Ave., go to the end and turn left onto Colchester Ave. The museum is about 200 yards farther

Hours: Mon.-Fri. 9-5, Sat., Sun. 1-5; closed on national holidays

Admission: Free. Ⓗ in progress

The present Neo-Classical building, dedicated in 1931 as a memorial to Robert Hull Fleming, an alumnus of the university, contains collections of art and archaeology, geology, paleontology, and natural history. It provides eight galleries on two floors adjoining a marble entrance court. The art collections have developed from an original "cabinet of curiosities" of 1826. While the Shelburne Museum surpasses them in the quality of its paintings and in American folk art, the Fleming Museum still ranks as the largest in Vermont and the one with the greatest coverage of world art. It is especially rich in the art of primitive cultures, and no other museum in the state regularly open to the public offers so rich a sampling of modern art.

Near the entrance the visitor will find a superb example of ancient Assyrian relief sculpture, a life-size image of a winged human deity from the Palace of Ashurnazirpal (883–859 B.C.). It is similar to reliefs from the same site owned by Amherst, Bowdoin, Dartmouth, Middlebury, and Williams colleges. The group as a whole is discussed in the section on Amherst College (MA 1).

A Gandharan *Head of the Buddha*, in black schist some 11 inches high, rivals in quality the full figure discussed at Yale University (CT 64).

The collection of so-called primitive art includes a wide range of examples from North, Central, and South America, Africa, the Asian mainland, the Philippines, and the South Pacific. Many were given by the painter Henry Schnakenberg, several of whose works are owned by the museum.

The masterpiece of this distinguished assemblage is a brass *Head of a Princess*[2] from Benin (Nigeria), of the sixteenth or seventeenth century.

2

The very broad collar extending to the mouth abruptly defines the cylindrical shape, while the conical hairdo, curving forward, echoes the prominent bulge of the forehead and the sharp projection of the nose. The features, simply delineated, are kept subordinate to the shape of the head as a whole. Most African sculpture is carved from wood, but the Benin kingdom, presumably under European influence, developed metal casting by the lost-wax process to a very high degree of craftsmanship. The classic description of the process itself is contained in the *Autobiography of Benvenuto Cellini* (Book II, chapters 75–78). The event —the casting of the *Perseus and Medusa*—occurred in 1550, but the manuscript was not published until 1728, well after the execution of the Benin sculptures. For Cellini, see MA 42; and for further discussion of the art of the Benin kingdom, see the section on the Peabody Museum of Harvard University.

The conical top of the Burlington head appears only on princesses (or queens). The head thus reaches a height of 15 inches, as against the 10½-inch height of an equally superb male example at the Peabody Museum. Both the neck and the Princess's high coiffure are bound in strands of coral; rosettes are set at her temples. As is customary in such heads, there is an opening at the top for the insertion of an elephant's tusk. During 1980 an exhibition, "Treasures of Ancient Nigeria: Legacy of 2,000 Years," selected by the Nigerian Federal Department of Antiquities, was shown in Detroit, San Francisco, and New York. It included heads of this kind, plaques like our MA 143, and work in terra-cotta, ivory, and stone. While Benin metal sculptures are generally referred to as bronzes, brass is a more accurate term.

Archaeological interests at the University of Vermont have not slighted local finds. The *Colchester Jar*,[3] discovered in 1825, came from a site less than ten miles north of Burlington. It was apparently left behind by New York Iroquois on a hunting trip to Vermont. In a letter of June 12, 1827, Luther Loomis described how it was found by Captain John Johnson "of whom I bought it yesterday. . . . If you think it worthy a place in the College of Nat. Hist. you will please accept it from your Humbl. Servt."

Such Indian pottery was made by the women, who used a paste of clay and powdered feldspar, mica, quartz, and other materials. When the basic shape of the jar was built up, it was finished with a finer clay

3

surface. After several days of drying, the design was scratched in, then fired.

The museum's extensive collection of paintings and drawings is strongest in the American field, but it includes two oils by Corot, a drawing of horses by Delacroix (and small bronzes by his colleague Barye—see VT 1), and English portraits by Michael Wright (seventeenth century), Kneller, Romney, Joseph Wright of Derby, and Lawrence, in addition to the Thomas Hudson *Portrait of Miss Ann Isted*,[4] which we now consider.

One of England's most influential painters, Hudson (1701–79) trained or indirectly affected the work of such varied talents as Sir Joshua Reynolds, Joseph Wright of Derby (see MA 152), and Joseph Blackburn (see ME 11), making his influence felt on both sides of the Atlantic. Yet his importance as a creative artist need not be exaggerated. To speak truthfully, his work is more competent than inspired. Hudson's rather tame variation on the prevalent Rococo style is nonetheless interesting because it demonstrates that the sources of High Georgian art were relatively plain and modest, as was likewise the case with painting in the American colony. Miss Isted's silver-gray dress with its blue ribbons contrasts well with the red chair and curtain, but without the intensity of John Singleton Copley (1738–1815). Copley's early career in Boston (see Deerfield, page 216) was developing at just the same time that Hudson painted Miss Isted (1756).

A portrait of about 1758 by John Wollaston well represents American Colonial painting, as do miniatures by James Peale and Edward G. Malbone in the Federal period. The mid-nineteenth-century Vermont portraitist Horace Bundy is seen in a characteristically sober pair. American landscape is here in some quantity, with good examples by Bierstadt, Blakelock, Cole, Sanford Gifford, Hinkley, and Wyant.

The Scratching Tree,[5] painted in 1848 by Thomas H. Hinkley (1813–1896), is composed like the idyllic pastoral scenes of the Hudson

4

5

River School, but its minuteness of detail and disarming insistence on what the bull is doing echo the work of such seventeenth-century Dutch painters as Paulus Potter, whose celebrated *Young Bull* (The Hague) has been aptly described as being as effective as it is prosaic. That Hinkley was subject to well-established formulae is shown by similarities between the Burlington landscape and one owned by Colby College, Waterville, Maine, painted in the following year.

As for the German-born American still-life painter Severin Roesen (active 1848–71), we have an embarrassment of riches as between the university's large *Fruit on Table*[6] and an equally fine version at the nearby Shelburne Museum. Little is known about Roesen's early training in his homeland, but his endless patience with detail seems a natural inheritance. Totally at variance with still lifes of such classic restraint as those of Chardin (see MA 216), and of such unobtrusiveness as those of Thomas Badger (see ME 36), Roesen gives us a galaxy that could be called Baroque were it not for the brittle edges and wiry precision of all these forms. Color runs to high intensities and rhythm to rapid movement. The wonder is that, turned upside down, the illustration shows that this profusion is visually coherent—that is, more than the sum of its parts.

From the American twentieth century you will find here drawings by Peggy Bacon and Isabel Bishop, a watercolor of 1915 by Charles Demuth (see MA 276), a pastel by Preston Dickinson, a wash drawing by William Kienbusch, several watercolors and drawings by Reginald Marsh (see VT 8) and by the Vermont painter-composer Carl Ruggles, and—from the very modern end of the spectrum—an oil by Ilya Bolotowsky (born 1907). *White Abstraction*,[7] 37 by 19 inches, painted in 1934/5, is published in Barbara Rose, *American Art Since 1900* (New York: Praeger, 1967, page 146). In the 1930s painters like Fritz Glarner and Josef Albers were also working in a vein distantly inspired by Piet Mondrian (see CT 85) and also related to compositions of the late 1920s by Pablo Picasso, such as *The Studio*, in the Museum of Modern Art. By the 1950s Bolotowsky moved closer to Glarner's so-called relational paintings (e.g., Glarner's enormous mural in the lobby of the Time-Life Building, New York City) and to their primal source, Piet Mondrian. Mondrian had led the way toward their own goal, an art totally divorced from the illusionistic representation of nature.

6

7

Southern Vermont Art Center

Location: Off West Road

Hours: July 4 to mid-October, Tues.-Sat. 10-5, Sun. 12-5; open Mon. if a holiday

Admission: Charged

The beautiful Manchester-Dorset region has long attracted artists of high competence and generally conservative stripe. A group of them incorporated in 1933 and inaugurated summer exhibitions that have become a major attraction of the area. In 1950 Southern Vermont Artists purchased their present attractive quarters, consisting of a large house and 375 acres with an imposing view eastward to the Green Mountains. Eleven of the original twenty-eight rooms were converted into galleries, and the studio-barn was refitted for classes in art instruction. In 1956 the Louise Ryals Arkell Pavilion opened for its annual series of musical concerts and film showings.

Through the years a permanent collection has been developed, with emphasis on the work of Vermont-associated painters, sculptors, print-makers, and photographers. Apart from Reginald Marsh, whom we shall discuss, the more established painters seen here are Carl Ruggles, Eugene Speicher, Peter Hurd, John Steuart Curry, Herbert Meyer, Dong Kingman, and Ogden Pleissner, whose large watercolor *Normandy Farm* is especially noteworthy. Sculptors include Simon Moselsio and Ossip Zadkine.

On the Bowery,[8] a 1946 watercolor and gouache measuring 27 by 40 inches, is a characteristically powerful work by Reginald Marsh (1898–1954) in a style developed in the Depression years that effectively expressed the prevailing spirit of the times. The New York Bowery became a favorite subject, and he never lost interest in it. Crowds of bathers at Coney Island also took on artistic significance under the magic of Marsh's brush. Unlikely as it may seem, both themes assumed a kind of grandeur under the inspiration of Michelangelo—not so much the Michelangelo of the Sistine Ceiling as the later and wilder Michelangelo of the *Last Judgment*. An ashen hue streaked with dissonant color, strong rhythmic connections between figures, and vigorous brushwork are major elements in Marsh's art.

8

The Johnson Gallery, Middlebury College

Location: At junction of Routes 7 and 30; turn west on Route 125 to bottom of hill below marble Catholic church, turn right, then second left up the hill to student parking lot B
Hours: Mon.-Fri., Sun. 12-5; Sat. 9-12, 1-5; closed during college vacations
Admission: Free. Ⓗ

Although Middlebury is one of New England's older colleges (opened 1800), its art museum is one of the youngest (opened 1968). An acquisition of the 1850s, an Assyrian relief from the Palace of Ashurnazirpal (see MA 1) is still shown in Munroe Hall rather than in the new gallery, where much of the available space is normally occupied by temporary exhibitions.

Near the museum entrance is a stainless-steel sculpture, 12 feet high, by George Rickey (see MA 163), *Two Open Rectangles/Excentric, Variation VI*, of 1976. Within, the permanent collection is strongest in small sculptures, of which we shall consider four examples. There are also landscapes by Kensett and Théodore Rousseau (Barbizon School, 1812–67); a landscape drawing by Fragonard; an extensive collection of Old Master and modern prints; African sculptures; and Far Eastern paintings, sculptures, and porcelains. A large sixteenth-century painting, *Judith with the Head of Holofernes*, is an interesting "problem piece": probably but not necessarily Italian, not authentic Bronzino or Parmigianino, yet impressive in design, drawing, and color. Like Pirandello's Six Characters, it is in search of an author.

In addition to our four sculpture selections, the following are noteworthy: the George Rickey already mentioned; a Calder mobile (*Black, Two Discs in Air*, c. 1960); a small South German wood *Madonna* of the first half of the eighteenth century; *Jaguar Devouring a Hare*, a bronze by Antoine Louis Barye (see VT 1); and a bronze cast of Falguière's *Diana*, of which we discuss the marble version at Wellesley College (MA 238).

In including the marble *Bust of the Greek Slave*,[9] by Hiram Powers

9

(born at Woodstock, Vt., 1805, died in Florence 1873), we make a flagrant exception to our policy to discuss only unique works of art. But the *Greek Slave* (marble of 1846 in the Corcoran Gallery, Washington; one of 1851 at Yale University; four others known, including the "original" of 1843 in an English private collection) was so popular that Powers and his many assistants were kept busy meeting the demand. The situation resembles that of Gilbert Stuart's "Athenaeum" Portraits of George Washington—the more so when we consider that the *Greek Slave* generated three additional marble replicas at two-thirds size (all posthumous, but carved by Powers's assistants), and the list of marble replicas of the bust reaches a total of no less than eighty in Donald M. Reynolds's doctoral thesis (Columbia University, 1975). At a height of 24 inches, these are at two-thirds the size of that portion of the original figure. Replicas identical to the Middlebury bust will be found at the Berkshire Museum, Pittsfield; the Addison Gallery of American Art, Andover; and a smaller one at the St. Johnsbury (Vt.) Athenaeum—to mention only New England collections open to the public.

However that may be, Hiram Powers is without much doubt Vermont's most distinguished sculptor, the *Greek Slave* is his most celebrated work, and he lived at a time when both sculptors and painters were delighted to keep abreast of the demand for replicas by employing specially trained assistants, usually adding final touches themselves to the approved product. Why, then, eliminate the *Greek Slave*?

We should note that Powers, like many ambitious Americans, established his studio abroad, and that from 1837 to his death he worked in Florence. If his glistening white nude females are safely within the Neoclassical formulae set by Antonio Canova and other sculptors well before 1800, they have an American air of bland moral purity, as if created by an artist determined not to be seduced like the mythical Pygmalion. To return to the question of mass production: Powers's signature, under the back, means only that the work came from his studio.

Head of a Gaul,[10] a fierce-looking bronze 14 inches high (including the base), is signed by the great progenitor of French Romantic sculpture, François Rude (1784–1855). His place in the history of sculpture is roughly equivalent to that of Théodore Géricault (1791–1824) in painting, except that Géricault's life was cut short much earlier. Comparison with the latter's *Madman-Kidnaper* (1822/3) at Springfield

10

(MA 218) or his wash drawing of a *Negro Soldier* at the Fogg Art Museum (MA 127) will illuminate the connection.

The plaster for the Middlebury head is in the Musée de Dijon, and illustrated in the handbook by P. Gasq and F. Marion (Paris: Henri Laurens, 1934, page 47). Dijon, where Rude was born, has in recent years remodeled a former Baroque church as a special and additional Rude Museum, and here can be seen full-scale plaster casts of his work, including one of his vast stone relief for the Arc de Triomphe in Paris, representing the *Departure of the Volunteers in 1792*. The Gaul in question is the main figure beneath the allegorical flying image of War. The great arch was originally commissioned by Napoleon in 1806, but not completed until 1836. Rude received the order for all four sculptures on the main facades, but through political intrigue three of them went to inferior competitors. Nevertheless, "La Marseillaise" commands the view as you approach up the Champs-Elysées, on the right side of the arch. Over 40 feet high, it was completed between 1833 and 1836. Whether Middlebury's obviously much smaller bronze of the Gaul's head was made from the original plaster model in Rude's lifetime, or later in the nineteenth century, is a specialist's problem that awaits solution. The demand for such small replicas was not of the immensity of that for the *Greek Slave*. If we break our general rule once again, by including this replica, our reason for doing so is partly that Rude's work is rarely seen in the United States, partly that the Arc de Triomphe relief is his masterpiece, partly that the Gaul's head dominates its exact center, and partly that the quality of this particular bronze is high. As in the case of Hiram Powers's *Bust of the Greek Slave*, the artist's signature is no guarantee that it was made in his lifetime.

With the *Head of Pierre de Wiessant*[11] by Auguste Rodin (1840–1917) we have no such problems. A cast in plaster and plasteline, it was given by Rodin himself to a friend, the engraver Jean Paricot. Numerous versions of this head exist in various sizes and media as studies for one of the six figures in Rodin's celebrated *Burghers of Calais*, a commission on which he worked from 1884 to 1887. The story of his trials and frustrations with the authorities of Calais, who desired a monument to

11

the city's heroic struggle against the English in the Hundred Years War, is recounted in detail by Albert Elsen in his *Rodin* (Museum of Modern Art, 1963). The installation, which did not take place until 1895, was doubly ironic. By an act of local pique, the group was not placed, as originally intended, in front of Calais's medieval town hall, but in a public garden; and elevated on a high pedestal, not on the tradition-breaking low base that Rodin rightly felt would emphasize the immediacy of his image. The six burghers who offered themselves as hostages to save their city were not allegorical abstractions, but local citizens. Not until 1926 was the monument placed where Rodin desired and on the low base he designed for it. A knoll in front of the town hall provides all the elevation it needs.

I have omitted so far any indication of the size of the Middlebury head. As I write these words, I am looking at an 8-by-10-inch photograph, and its impact is nothing less than majestic. The same is true of the work itself, although it measures less than 4 inches in height. From the 85-inch height of the final monument, I estimate the head of Pierre de Wiessant at about 12 inches. Except for its size, it resembles Middlebury's little masterpiece with minor differences. A date of close to 1884 seems appropriate for the latter. On page 75 of his *Rodin*, Elsen illustrates a bronze version of the head at heroic size, owned by the Cleveland Museum of Art, which he dates as "by 1889." In other words, this particular head is probably an "afterthought"—of the same character as various heads by Picasso that followed his mural painting of 1937, *Guernica*, and not to be confused with the many studies that preceded that great composition. The Cleveland head carries the expression of inner torment still further than the Middlebury head or the figure in the completed monument. The sequence here is paralleled in Rodin's *Walking Man* (MA 190), developed from an earlier figure, as we have seen in the section on the Smith College Museum of Art. At three greatly differing sizes—under 4 inches (Middlebury), about 12 inches (completed monument), and 32 inches (Cleveland)—the head of Pierre de Wiessant remains faithful to Rodin's early conception of it and yet becomes more deeply expressive. At whatever size he worked, however, Rodin's imagination operated on a plane of grandeur.

Bimbo Malato (*Sick Child*),[12] a wax over plaster bust of 1893 by Medardo Rosso, completes our survey of Middlebury's small but dis-

12

tinguished group of sculptures. Born in Turin in 1858 and working in Paris in the 1880s and 1890s, Rosso had a relationship with Rodin, his senior by eighteen years, that has puzzled and intrigued scholars for a long time. We know that he arrived in Paris in 1884, became an assistant to Dalou (see MA 239), and met Rodin; that he soon returned to Milan (where he had grown up and received early training) but exhibited at the annual Paris Salons; that by 1889 he was back in Paris; that in 1894 Rodin wrote him an enthusiastic letter after visiting his studio; and that from 1890 to 1910 Rosso enjoyed an international reputation second only to Rodin's. When Rodin exhibited his plaster of the final (clothed) version of the *Balzac*, Rosso became convinced that Rodin "had taken a great deal" from him. This charge, otherwise unspecified, did not improve the relationship; but it is possible that it contained a general truth. A look through Margaret Scolari Barr's book on Rosso (Museum of Modern Art, 1963) will demonstrate similarities in the Impressionistic surfaces and the shadowy-garbed figures of the period 1893 to 1895. On the other hand, Rosso's debt to Rodin from the very outset of his career is obvious. What seems to have happened is that a normal relationship between two highly gifted artists was spoiled by lack of generosity on the part of an older titan and by hypersensitivity on the part of the younger man.

However that may be, Middlebury has been fortunate in acquiring Rosso's haunting image of a sick child, one that would make an interesting comparison with Edvard Munch's various representations in oil and lithography of his invalid sister—beginning as early as 1885. Rosso's special technique of modeling the top surfaces in wax over a plaster base is wonderfully appropriate for expressing impermanence and flux; but the moment in time that he caught was not joyous, as in the paintings of the Impressionists, but one of tormented uncertainty and disintegration—an Impressionist technique, but used for Expressionist ends. It does not seem irrelevant to add that Middlebury's bust was once owned by the philosopher Ludwig Josef Johann Wittgenstein.

Sheldon Museum

Location: Park Street

Hours: June to the end of September, Mon.-Sat. 10-5; October to the end of May, Tues. and Thurs. 1-5; closed Sundays

Admission: Charged

The museum was founded by Henry Sheldon in 1881 in an early nineteenth-century brick house, to exhibit Vermont life at various times in its history. A modern rearrangement includes paintings and furnishings from about 1780 to about 1890. There is an emphasis on folkways, on the tools people have used, the clothes they wore, their books, games, medicines; on the essentials and the trivia of human existence.

From the point of view of the present book, the most interesting items are two portraits by William Jennys, who flourished in the Connecticut River Valley in the 1790s and early 1800s, of the wife and the daughter of Gamaliel Painter, a founder of Middlebury College. There is also a modern copy of Jennys's portrait of Painter himself, of which the original hangs in the office of the president of the college. We have discussed this expressive portraitist in examples at New London (CT 87) and Manchester (NH 17), and outlined his connection with Richard Jennys, who was either his father or older brother, in the section on the Connecticut Historical Society. It is interesting to find him working as far north as central Vermont.

Behind the museum a well-appointed research library serves students and scholars.

Thomas Waterman Wood Art Gallery

Location: Kellogg-Hubbard Library, 135 Main Street
Hours: Tues.-Sat. 12-4; in summer, Tues.-Fri. 12-4, Sat. 9-1
Admission: Free

More than a hundred paintings by the Montpelier painter Thomas Waterman Wood (1823–1903) are preserved here. After training under Chester Harding and study in Paris, Wood practiced in New York and as far afield as Kentucky before returning to Montpelier, where he opened a gallery to exhibit his own work and that of some of his contemporaries. The collection was moved from Wood's old house to the second floor of the Kellogg-Hubbard Library. In addition to works by nineteenth-century painters like Asher Durand and Alexander Wyant, the collection now includes paintings by such twentieth-century artists as Joseph Stella and Reginald Marsh (see VT 8).

Wood specialized in portraiture and genre scenes. His hard style of painting and his observant eye were well suited to his descriptive intention.

The Vermont Museum

Location: 109 State Street (near the state capitol)
Hours: Mon.-Fri. 8-4:30, except legal holidays; during July, August, and foliage season also open Sat., Sun. 10-5
Admission: Free ("small donation appreciated"). Ⓗ by Taylor St. entrance

Described as "a history museum dedicated to telling the Vermont story," The Vermont Museum succeeds admirably in fulfilling that task. It is housed on the first floor of the New Pavilion, built soon after the razing of the old, mansard-roofed Pavilion Hotel, of 1870 vintage, and designed to resemble it. The Vermont Historical Society moved its headquarters here in 1971, and for the first time in its 138 years of existence had a museum properly equipped to display its wide-ranging collections. These include some good portraits from the first half of the nineteenth century, country furniture, textiles, glass, pottery, and metalware.

The rear of the exhibition area opens onto the foyer of a modern office building, and here—as well as in the nearby state-capitol complex —you will find modern paintings and sculptures acquired by the Vermont Council on the Arts. A large landscape, *Champlain Valley* (1976/7, 33 by 84 inches) by Thelma Appel, who worked in the Bennington area for some years before moving to New York City, achieves the difficult combination of surface interest through linear brush strokes and an impression of deep space without resort to perspective or a horizon line. The range of color is exhilarating, as fresh as a Schubert song.

Elsewhere in the complex is a big stainless-steel sculpture[13] by Isaac Witkin (born 1936), formerly a member of the art faculty of Bennington College, but now centered in New York. *Spill XII*, measuring

13

76 by 116 inches in height and width, dates from 1976. Designed like rings of fire receding in depth, it is one of a series utilizing spills collected from a steel factory and assembled according to the dictates of the artist's imagination. The elements are patinated with varying acid combinations to produce colors and textures that have the appearance of being brushed as in a painting. Witkin has exhibited widely and enjoys an international reputation. Other examples of his work are at the Massachusetts Institute of Technology, the Hirshhorn Museum in Washington, and the Tate Gallery in London.

Locations of works acquired by the Vermont Council on the Arts are subject to change, and inquiry at its offices at 136 State Street (not far from The Vermont Museum) is advisable.

The St. Johnsbury Athenaeum and Art Gallery

Location: 30 Main Street at Eastern Avenue, junction of U.S. 2 and U.S. 5
Hours: Mon. and Fri. 10-8, Tues.-Thurs. 10-5, Sat. 10-2
Admission: Free

The handsome library building, completed in 1871 from designs by John Davis Hatch of New York, and its gallery wing, completed two years later, were the gift of Governor Horace Fairbanks, whose fortune derived from the invention of the platform scale by Thaddeus Fairbanks of St. Johnsbury. While the Art Gallery is not the oldest in the United States—the gallery of the Wadsworth Atheneum in Hartford, for example, dates from 1842—it may well be the oldest still in its original form.

An attractive illustrated catalogue of the collection lists some ninety paintings and nine marbles. With paintings superimposed two and three deep and some displayed on easels, and with mauve-textured walls broken by dark green pilasters ornamented in gold with classical motifs, the ensemble sets a tone that has strong nostalgic appeal in an age accustomed to antiseptic white backgrounds and dramatic isolation of individual works. The small white marbles provide sparkling accents in the generally dark scheme.

The entire end wall is occupied by a major work of Albert Bierstadt (1830–1902), whom we have seen in early pastorals at Framingham (MA 154) and the Fruitlands Museum at Harvard (MA 158), and in the operatic *Seal Rock*, of 1872, at New Britain (CT 44). *Domes of the Yosemite*,[14] nearly 10 feet high and 15 feet long (without frame), was painted in 1867. Governor Fairbanks acquired it from a New York collector, and it has dominated the gallery ever since. Bierstadt traveled to the Far West in 1863 with Fitz Hugh Ludlow, and Ludlow described their adventures in the *Atlantic Monthly* for June of the following year. His response to the Yosemite was cleary shared by Bierstadt: "I never could call a Yosemite crag inorganic, as I used to speak of everything not strictly animal or vegetable. In the presence of the Great South Dome that utterance became blasphemous." From his many oil studies made on the spot, Bierstadt developed a long series of Yosemite can-

14

vases; it is estimated that over a quarter of his finished paintings were devoted to that subject. An earlier view, more peaceful and taken at a greater distance from the crags (1866), is owned by the Wadsworth Atheneum, Hartford. In the summer of 1873 Bierstadt, with his wife and a few friends, spent several weeks camping in and around Hetch-Hetchy Valley, some fifty miles north of the Yosemite. Of the many paintings resulting from that trip, examples can be seen at Hartford and at the Mount Holyoke College Art Museum (see page 280).

It must be acknowledged that Bierstadt depended heavily on the impressiveness of his subjects, and that his paintings seldom reached the poetic intensity of Frederic Church's, as seen at the Berkshire Museum, Pittsfield, M A 195. One of the few disappointments in St. Johnsbury's fine collection of painters associated with the Hudson River School is the absence of a work by this master.

Jasper Cropsey (1823–1900), born on Staten Island, N.Y., took two long European trips for study in Italy and England before settling at Hastings-on-Hudson. Besides painting on the Hudson and the Susquehanna and in the Catskills and the White Mountains, he frequented Lake Greenwood and the Ramapo Valley on the New Jersey–New York border. *Autumn on the Ramapo River*,[15] 37 by 64 inches and painted in 1876, is a lovely idyll of the season he liked best, when the fall foliage gave him an opportunity to indulge his passion for rich reds, dappled on in quick small strokes. (At Hartford, however, there is a *Winter Scene* painted in the Ramapo area.) Comparison with Corot's *Grez-sur-Loing: Bridge and Church*, at the Currier Gallery, Manchester (N H 26), will show the great difference between American interest in poetic light and Romantic love of nature, and French concern with compositional structure. Corot's bridge is a rhythm of strong shapes and a connector between the two sides of his painting; Cropsey's, a flimsy support for a diminutive couple engaged, no doubt, in amorous dialogue. The Currier Gallery owns another fine Cropsey, but of nearly twenty years earlier, *Indian Summer Morning in the White Mountains*.

Cropsey's contemporary Sanford R. Gifford (1823–80) grew up in Hudson, N.Y., just across the river from Catskill, where Thomas Cole (1801–48) maintained a studio. *South Mountain, Catskills*,[16] 23 by 40 inches, was painted in 1873. The horizontal format is typical of the work of Gifford, who preferred wide panoramas to towering masses. His extraordinary sensitiveness to effects of light has been mentioned in connection with examples at New Bedford and in the George Walter Vincent Smith Museum at Springfield, Mass. Like Martin Heade and

15

Fitz Hugh Lane, he was one of our visual poets. Gifford's early work shows the influence of Cole, but gradually his forms became dissolved in a new radiance. Like Bierstadt, with whom he traveled in Europe in the 1850s, and like Church, he sought out exotic scenery, venturing as far afield as Turkey and Syria, the Rockies, and Alaska. But Gifford's was a calm spirit, to whom aqueous mirages and luminous skies spoke more directly than scenic wonders.

A historical curiosity here is a dozen or more nineteenth-century copies made in the European galleries of works by Andrea del Sarto, Raphael, Paolo Veronese, Guido Reni, Carlo Dolci, Fra Angelico, Van Dyck, Murillo, and—surprisingly—Rosa Bonheur. Such copies, often well painted, were regular fixtures in museums of the time, but they are rarely seen today.

As for the St. Johnsbury marbles, most are anonymous but have the appeal of subjects like Psyche, Hermes, Venus, Diana, and Julius Caesar. But the prominent Neoclassicist Antonio Canova (1757–1822) is represented by a *Dancing Girl* (height about 20 inches), and Vermont's own Hiram Powers by yet another bust of the *Greek Slave* (this example only 13½ inches high), discussed at Middlebury College (VT 9). Another good American sculptor, John Quincy Adams Ward (1830–1910), is represented by a portrait of special local interest: Governor Horace Fairbanks himself.

16

Shelburne Museum

Location: On U.S. Route 7, about 7 miles south of the center of Burlington. Parking available

Hours: 9-5 daily from mid-May to mid-October

Admission: Charged (two-day tickets can be purchased). Ⓗ

A full day, or two days, for an unhurried visit to this superb enterprise will be well repaid in interest, aesthetic delight, and educational value. There are thirty-five buildings to inspect, most of them full of art or artifacts, on forty-five acres of parklike setting of fruit trees, formal gardens, and well-tended lawns. At the Toll Booth and Information Center a useful map is provided.

The Shelburne Museum was founded in 1947 by Mr. and Mrs. J. Watson Webb to preserve Vermont's traditions of building and craftsmanship. Like the marine museum at Mystic, Conn., it is not a static display, nor is it a reconstruction of a vanished town in the manner of Colonial Williamsburg. Described as a "collection of collections," it is enlivened by things to do as well as to see, and by skilled guides and craftsmen from whom one may learn much. Installations combine the highest order of historical accuracy and good taste. The care for detail is extraordinary, and it extends to the hundreds of explanatory labels. Indeed, many an established museum of fine arts could profit from a study of methods used here to develop effective public education.

First of all, the museum is a collection of buildings of the eighteenth and nineteenth centuries: houses, barns, an inn, a meetinghouse, a school, a lighthouse, a jail, a blacksmith shop, a general store, a railroad station, a Shaker shed, and a covered bridge. Almost all of these came from Vermont sites—some ten from Shelburne itself or nearby Charlotte, and frequently saved thereby from imminent destruction. Endleaf pictorial maps in the superbly illustrated book *A Pictorial History of the Shelburne Museum* (Shelburne, Vermont: Shelburne Museum, 1972), show the original locations.

Second, the museum is a collection of American crafts exhibited in appropriate architectural settings: interior decoration and furnishings, household utensils, rugs, quilts, pewter, glass, and ceramics. Third, it contains what is probably the finest collection of native American sculpture in existence. Fourth, it is a museum of transportation, with an outstanding collection of luxury carriages, coaches, wagons, sleighs, and of horse-drawn fire equipment; and of ship models, ship paintings, and marine prints. Poised at the Shelburne Depot is an engine and the private car "Grand Isle," built about 1890 by the Wagner Palace Car Company and presented by its president, Dr. W. Seward Webb (the father of J. Watson Webb), to the governor of Vermont, Edward C. Smith. It contains an observation room, two staterooms, a parlor, a secretary's stateroom, a porter's room, and a kitchen. Mahogany paneling and furnishings are in the best style of the period. Not far away is the

892-ton side-wheeler *Ticonderoga*,[17] hauled two miles overland to its present resting place and imaginatively tilted to give you the feeling, on board, that you are under way. *Ticonderoga*'s engine was built at Hoboken, N.J., by Andrew Fletcher and Sons; her hull, by T. S. Marvel on the Hudson River and shipped to Lake Champlain by the Champlain Canal; and her joiner work was completed in 1905 at the Shelburne Harbor Shipyard of the Champlain Transportation Company. She plied the lake from 1906 to 1953.

Metal weather vanes, wood figures for commercial enterprises, and ship's figureheads rival those discussed elsewhere in this book. While sculpture was the slowest of the visual arts to develop in the American colonies and the early Republic—no doubt because of its relative infrequency in English art and because of the Puritans' fear of idolatry—it would be easy to exaggerate its rarity. We must keep in mind, however, that until about 1850 it was almost entirely utilitarian.

The Stagecoach Inn houses a varied supply of weather vanes, cigarstore figures, trade signs, circus figures, symbolic eagles, and ship's figureheads. Most of the weather vanes take the form of an animal: a horse, ram, boar, cow, fish, butterfly, peacock. Occasionally the human figure appears: an Indian archer, a classical centaur, a mermaid. The railroad engine was also a popular theme; a sheet-zinc example here includes a brass and iron lightning-rod attachment above the smokestack. Found in Rhode Island, it is thought to have been used on a railroad station. Whether this object was cut flat from sheet metal or hammered into half-round relief, its silhouette against the sky was its chief visual element. The artisan simplified his forms with an unerring eye for clarity and expressiveness.

The making of bird decoys gave the carver further opportunities to set down characteristic positions of head and body. A collection of over a thousand of these decoys is shown in Dorset House, near the covered bridge. Of special delight for circus lovers is the Circus Parade, stretching more than five hundred feet around the interior of a horseshoe-shaped building near the Shelburne Depot. Carved and painted by Roy Arnold and four other craftsmen over a period of many years were sixty Lilliputian bandwagons, cage wagons, and other spectaculars, some 450 horses (no two alike), animals, riders, clowns, and musicians. On the walls is a running display of posters that cover the history of the American circus.

The exterior of public buildings gave the carver his most challenging opportunity. The great wooden eagles were, so to speak, decoys raised

17

to the level of fine art. One of them with a wingspread of sixteen feet
(shown in the Stagecoach Inn) came from the Marine Base at Portsmouth, N.H. More rarely the human figure was employed. The per-
sonification of Justice,[18] 10 feet high, that greets you in the entrance
hall of the Webb Gallery once adorned the top of the courthouse at
Barnstable, Mass. Carved from pine, the blindfolded figure holds a
metal scale and a sword. Its rough planes give it unusual vigor; and
both the subject and the date of c. 1800 make it extremely rare. In 1958
Justice was exhibited at the Brussels Universal and International Exposition in the section on American art.

In the entry for Old Deerfield we have discussed rather briefly the
emergence of quilting as an American art form (see MA 149).
Throughout the Shelburne Museum one becomes increasingly aware of
the American artist's sensibility to shape and color, but especially in
rug design and in the elaborate productions of the quilting bee. The
textile display in the Hat and Fragrance Unit (beyond the Stagecoach
Inn at the northern end of the museum) is very large, and the quilts
and coverlets are as magnificent in design as they are spectacular in
workmanship. Perhaps the most extraordinary of the quilts is the *Star of
Bethlehem*,[19] almost 9 feet square (partly turned under at the bottom
of our illustration). Its date is thought to be early nineteenth century.
The appliqué design is made of a patchwork of chintzes and English
calicos in a symmetrical pattern. Diamond-shaped pieces in the border
are made of the same materials. The corner squares are fashioned of
cutout chintz on a white background. Three bands of yellow and red
material worked with a design of interlaced circles form the wide border,
together with the diamond-shaped pieces already mentioned. As would
be expected in such a virtuoso performance, the quilting of the background is superbly managed.

Earlier in this account of the museum, we listed four types of collections. We turn now to two others, which from the point of view of
this book are the most important of all. In 1960 the Webb Gallery
opened as a showcase for the collection of American paintings that Mrs.

18

19

Webb assembled while amassing the many thousands of pieces of Americana that fill the various buildings here. In the same year, 1960, Mr. and Mrs. Webb died. She had inherited from her parents, Henry O. and Louisine Havemeyer, an important share of their magnificent collection of European art, the bulk of which went to the Metropolitan Museum of Art in New York—one of the greatest acquisitions in its history. Mrs. Webb had long planned to bring to Shelburne what remained of this inheritance after further gifts by the Havemeyers' children to expand the great bequest to the Metropolitan. Her own children decided instead to create a memorial to their mother by installing the present collection exactly as it appeared in the Webbs' Park Avenue apartment. Six rooms were reconstructed in a fine new building of Greek Revival style overlooking the southern end of the museum complex, not far from the Webb Gallery. The Electra Havemeyer Webb Memorial opened in 1967.

As a result of these two additions, Shelburne became the leading art museum of the state of Vermont—though its range is much more limited than the collections of the nearby University of Vermont—and indeed one of the finest in New England outside the great cities. From these riches we have selected four masterpieces of French nineteenth-century art (works by Corot, Courbet, Manet, and Degas) and two American paintings of high quality (by Peto and Wyeth). As always in our survey of a collection of great importance, limitations of space have proved constricting and our selections have had to fit into an overall plan to present a well-rounded picture of the history of art.

Two Rembrandt portraits in the living room of the apartment, dating from 1632 and 1643, make a good appearance but cannot match the examples discussed at the Gardner Museum (MA 48) and the Fogg Art Museum (MA 124). A *Portrait of the Princess de la Paz*, in one of the bedrooms, is close to Goya, but because of a certain flatness and lack of spirit it is merely attributed to him. Mary Cassatt's pastel *Portrait of Mrs. Henry O. Havemeyer* (1899), hanging nearby, has greater energy. Artist and subject were close friends, and it was Cassatt (see CT 98) who advised the Havemeyers in their collecting activities in Paris, especially in the field of nineteenth-century French art.

Greek Girl: Mademoiselle Dobigny,[20] by Jean Baptiste Camille Corot (1796–1875), about 33 inches high, is probably unsurpassed among

20

the many late figure paintings of this artist. The date is c. 1868–70. It has been widely exhibited: at Chicago, the New York World's Fair (1940), Philadelphia, the Louvre, and the Metropolitan Museum of Art, among other places. Emma Dobigny, one of Corot's favorite models, posed for it. Fugitive colors animate a predominantly grayish picture, and fugitive also is the girl's facial expression. The forms are softly rounded, yet structurally firm. In this Vermeer-like world of silence, it is hard to believe that the artist was an almost exact contemporary of Delacroix (see MA 120) and an exact one of the sculptor Barye (see VT 1).

Our next two selections, *Still Life with Fruit*[21] by Gustave Courbet (1819–77) and *Blue Venice*[22] by Edouard Manet, both about 22 by 28 inches, are paired on a landing of the memorial's beautiful staircase. For his alleged activities in the destruction of the Vendôme Column in Paris during the Commune uprising, Courbet was sentenced to six months in the Ste.-Pélagie prison. He was confined there from September to December 1871, but because of illness he was allowed to serve the remainder of his term at a Neuilly clinic. Although the Shelburne picture is signed and inscribed "71 Ste. Pélagie," it is possible that it was painted at Neuilly and so inscribed to advertise what Courbet considered a gross miscarriage of justice. One such still life, so inscribed, was scornfully rejected at the Salon of 1872. During his confinement Courbet could paint only fruit or flowers (although there is a self-portrait from this time), because he was one of those rare artists of genius who are helpless unless the motif, or its elements, is literally in front of their eyes. Some of the Ste.-Pélagie or Neuilly still lifes, stark and devoid of accessories, rival the solemnity and geometrical purity of Chardin and Cézanne. Others, like the Shelburne picture, are given landscape backgrounds and otherwise encumbered. The weakest part of

21

22

this picture is the landscape, precisely because Courbet had to imagine it. In his violent espousal of the doctrine of Realism each tangible object reinforced his stand; as a result, there is often a plethora of forms. The basket here is indeed heavily laden. Color is much stronger than in the Smith College picture of almost twenty years earlier (MA 178). By 1871/2 the much younger Impressionists were emerging; while they were greatly influenced by Courbet's themes and by his application of heavy masses of the oil medium, it is very doubtful that their color had much interest for him. As for Courbet's later years, he spent the last five of them in exile in Switzerland, out of touch with what was happening in Paris.

What was happening in Paris was the First and Second Impressionist exhibitions (1874 and 1876), Renoir's *Moulin de la Galette* (Louvre), and boating pictures painted at Argenteuil by Renoir, Monet (RI 16), and Manet, whose *Boating at Argenteuil*, exhibited at the 1874 official Salon, was eventually bequeathed to the Metropolitan Museum of Art by the Havemeyers. In the early fall of 1875, Edouard Manet (1832–83) visited Venice in the company of James Tissot (see RI 19) and brought back two magnificent scenes of the Grand Canal. A vertical canvas, 23 by 19 inches, is in San Francisco; Mrs. Webb's *Blue Venice*, of similar height but 28½ inches wide, is more daring in its elimination of the conventional sky and in its concentration on water reflections, the blue-striped mooring poles, and a shining black gondola placed at the very center. This picture was once owned by Tissot and it has been exhibited many times—in Paris, New York, and especially at the major Manet retrospective of 1966/7 at Philadelphia and Chicago. Black contrasted with prismatic colors: that is Manet's forte—black inherited from Courbet but more directly inspired by Velázquez, black continued from Manet's own pictures of the 1860s (CT 2). In the distance, not the expected hues of Renoir and Monet, but earth-browns and whites. In his turn to Impressionism he remained faithful to the work of those earlier years, but what a dazzling maze of brush strokes in the new Impressionist technique!

Edgar Degas (1834–1917), a great favorite of the Havemeyers, is seen here in four superb pictures, especially the whitish vision of *Two Ballet Girls* in the living room, and in a bronze cast of *The Little Dancer, Age Fourteen*,[23] about 38 inches high. A similar cast is in the

23

Clark Art Institute, Williamstown, and others are in major museums in the United States. The original wax version dates from 1880; the Shelburne bronze, purchased by Mrs. Webb, is the tenth of an edition of twenty-two cast by the Paris foundry of Hébrard in 1922. We should not forget that, as in the case of sculpture by Honoré Daumier, all Degas bronzes are posthumous.

The original wax figure, now in the collection of Mr. and Mrs. Paul Mellon, Upperville, Va., was listed for inclusion in the Impressionist exhibition of 1880, but as it was not completed in time, Degas exhibited it the following year. The ballerina was dressed in a real bodice, a white muslin tutu, a wig (probably of horsehair), a blue satin ribbon tied around her pigtail, and satin slippers. All these additions except the tutu and the slippers were coated with wax to make their texture agree with the rest of the figure, and this also facilitated the later casting. On the advice of Mary Cassatt, the Havemeyers sought to purchase it, but negotiations with Degas broke down; in due course they acquired the first bronze cast in the Hébrard edition of twenty-two. That cast was given to the Metropolitan Museum of Art.

No less than seventy-two wax figures by Degas were cast at the Hébrard foundry between 1919 and 1922. Except for *The Little Dancer* and a nude study for it of the same size (a cast of the nude version is in the Albright-Knox Gallery, Buffalo), these were figurines that Degas used as models for paintings of ballet subjects and racing pictures. According to the contract between Degas's heirs and the Hébrards, the wax originals became the property of the foundry. Until the 1950s it was thought that they were lost, but discovery that they had survived the German occupation of Paris in the Second World War in the basement of the Hébrard house led to their exhibition, for the first time ever, in 1955 at the Knoedler Galleries in New York. While their dull finish could not match the glint of light that animates the bronzes, the extreme subtlety of their surfaces was a revelation, surpassing even the expertly cast replicas.

In the bronze versions, the tutu (again a real one) has turned a dirty greenish gray, and the real hair ribbon was sometimes omitted, or subsequently lost. Chemical patination successfully reproduced the already oxidized tones of the original wax, especially in the bodice area. A fine account of *The Little Dancer* is in John Rewald, *Degas: Sculpture* (London: Thames & Hudson, 1957), which contains six superb plates of the dressed figure and two of the nude version. Rewald points out that the developments of Degas and Renoir were diametrically opposed —Renoir moving away from Impressionism toward firmer line, Degas toward increasingly pictorial effects. He quotes a penetrating statement about the *Dressed Dancer* by Sacha Guitry: ". . . a kind of hallucinating mummy . . . You would have to go a long way, a very long way, right to Egypt and into its ancient past to discover a work of art to equal her."

A large still life in the Webb Gallery, 56 by 33 inches and signed "John F. Peto/ 1887," bears the title *Ordinary Objects in the Artist's Creative Mind*.[24] The title is an accurate statement of the credo of John Frederick Peto (1854–1907): homely objects elevated to the plane of art. A green door with rusty locks and hinges serves as background for

a blue-covered book, a photograph of a woman, a wood engraving of a
boy and girl on a beach (by Winslow Homer, appearing years before
in *Harper's* magazine), a canvas still life of Peto's with edges curled
out, a music book with a torn reddish cover, a trumpet (on which Peto
played expertly), and a sign AT DINNER hanging from a nail. This
modest assemblage agrees entirely with the character of Peto's *Discarded
Treasures* at Smith College (MA 187), returned, as we have indicated, to
Peto's oeuvre despite its Harnett signature. It contrasts strikingly with
the luxurious array of objects in Harnett's *Emblems of Peace* at Springfield (MA 220). Both these Philadelphians were masters at fooling the
eye, but Harnett's choice of objects aimed at attracting affluent patrons
and as a result he had a much greater success. He often influenced Peto,
six years his junior, nowhere more so than in the Shelburne picture,
which may be called a poor man's version of Harnett's relatively elegant
After the Hunt (1885, at the California Palace of the Legion of Honor,
San Francisco). While it is clear that Harnett was the more expert
composer, in the tattered array that Peto has given us, a new note of
pessimism prevails. This has been remarked upon by Gerdts and Burke
in *American Still Life Painting* (New York: Praeger, 1971), and by
Alfred Frankenstein in *After the Hunt* (Berkeley: University of California Press, 1953) with his apt phrase, "the pathos of the discarded."

At the Payson Gallery in Portland, we shall encounter Andrew Wyeth
(born 1917) in an early tempera landscape of 1940 (ME 20).
Shelburne owns one of his most impressive works, painted ten years
later. *Soaring*,[25] tempera on Masonite, is 4 feet high and more than 7
feet wide. A huge brown-black turkey vulture—one soon discovers two

24

25

others far below—straddles most of the picture surface, wings out-stretched on a dramatic diagonal. A diminutive house and shed inform us of the vulture's great altitude, but without distracting from the force of Wyeth's flat design. Spears of deep brown woodland project into the bare gray-greenish-ochered fields and unobtrusively echo the vulture's shape—all this beneath a narrow ice-pale sky. Gone are the rich Burgundy reds of 1940 and even the forlorn pink of the dress in *Christina's World*, 1948 (Museum of Modern Art)—still, in the opinion of many, Wyeth's finest work. Since 1950, Wyeth has continued in the dour vein and tonality of *Soaring*, at times repetitiously—as appears when a great number of his pictures are shown together—but often striking deep emotional chords. As for *Soaring*, it deserves comparison with the great gilded eagle in the Stagecoach Inn, carved by an anonymous craftsman perhaps a century ago. Power triumphant there (and then); in Wyeth, power turned gloomy and ominous.

Springfield Art and Historical Society

Location: 9 Elm Hill. From I-91 take exit 11 or 12 onto Route 11 into Springfield. Beyond the center of town look for a right turn up a steep hill onto Elm St., and then take the *first* right turn onto Elm Hill and destination. Follow these directions with care! Parking available

Hours: Mon.-Fri. 12-4:30, weekends by appointment

Admission: Free

As I near the end of this book, it is a pleasure to make an appeal to the public-spirited reader to support a deserving institution. Springfield is not a large town, and the existence of the Art and Historical Society does it credit. Nevertheless, the handsome building of the 1860s, given in 1956 by Mr. and Mrs. Edward W. Miller, needs considerable repair, and a number of the good pictures it contains are in dire need of a conservator's tender, loving, and expensive care.

Other than the paintings and objects of primarily historical interest, the collections include Bennington pottery, pewter by Richard Lee, dolls, toys, quilts, and costumes. Of special local interest, but now gaining increasing attention, are four portraits of the Chase family by Asahel Lynde Powers (1800–81), a native of Springfield who also painted in New York State and in Ohio. Powers was brought from obscurity by the American specialist Jean Lipman, in an article in *Antiques* for June 1959, and in her subsequent books on American painting. The New York Historical Association at Cooperstown (more often visited than Springfield) has Powers's *Portrait of Charles Mortimer French as a Child*, painted in 1839, some seven years after the Chase portraits, but folk-art enthusiasts should see the examples in Springfield itself to gain a more extended impression of this artist's uncouth, but strangely provocative, forms. His combination of different perspectives has an unexpectedly modern air; and if his deeply lined facial features make every person, regardless of age, seem venerable, Asahel Powers was by no means unique in this respect.

Another Vermont artist, better known than Asahel Powers, is Horace Bundy (1814–83), who came from Hardwick. A portrait and sometime landscape painter in Vermont and New Hampshire, he was in Jamaica shortly before his death, on commission by an English planter. There he also made sketches of tropical scenery. A portrait of 1841, *A Vermont Lawyer*, in the Garbisch collection at the National Gallery of Art in Washington, which is among his best works, is generally comparable to one of 1845 at Springfield. Bundy has received much attention from scholars and collectors in the American field, and his career is now well established. Springfield owns seven of his portraits and a landscape.

Bundy Art Gallery

Location: On Route 100 about 4 miles south of the village. From I-93 turn south on Route 100 at Waterbury. Parking available
Hours: Open July and August, Mon., Wed.-Sat. 10-5, Sun. 1-5
Admission: Free

Described as a country museum dedicated to contemporary art, European as well as American, the gallery was founded and designed by Harlow Carpenter and named in memory of his mother, Helen Bundy Carpenter. It opened in 1962.

Modern sculptures, many of them placed on the grounds and along paths and in clearings of the beautiful woodland property, include works by Dino Basaldella, Roger Bolomey, Luciano Minguzzi, Louise Nevelson (see MA 147), and Sahl Swarz. Among well-known modern painters represented here by major works are Afro (Basaldella), Karel Appel, John Grillo, Ivor Hitchens, Conrad Marca-Relli, Pierre Soulages, Janis Spyropoulos, Antoni Tapiès, and Esteban Vicente.

Changing exhibitions feature selections from the large permanent collection and work by avant-garde Vermont artists. Free concerts are also a part of the gallery's program.

Maine

Maine

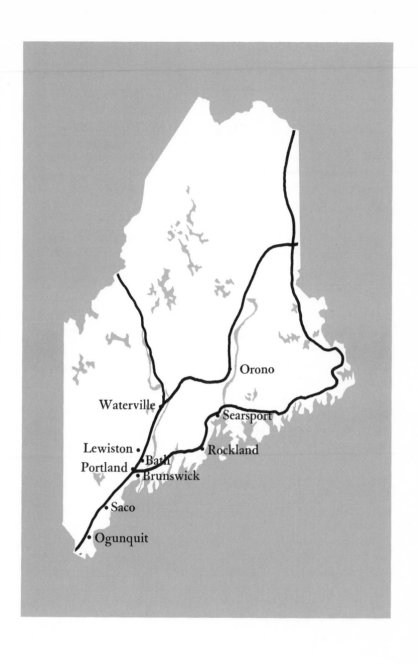

Maine Maritime Museum

Location: 963 Washington St. Take Maine Tpke. exit 9 for coastal Route 1
through Brunswick to Bath; take exit 209 from Route 1 onto High St., which
parallels Washington St.; turn left (north) on Washington St. Sewall House
is at the near right corner of North St.

Hours: Daily 10-5 from mid-May to late October; after that on Sun. 10-5

Admission: Charged

The museum occupies Sewall House, a superb mansion of 1844,
and, with additions, provides 5,600 square feet of space for exhibition
of the maritime collections. Ship models are here, 200 of them, from
early sailing craft to J. P. Morgan's *Corsair* (3,100 tons)—built at the
Bath Iron Works—to ships built for the U.S. Navy. Bath is the oldest
still active shipbuilding city in the United States. The basement of
Sewall House has been admirably fitted out for exhibition of these
modern activities.

There are a few carved ships' figureheads, but not of the magnitude
of those at Mystic Seaport. The many maritime paintings are of high
quality. One of the most interesting represents the U.S. ship *Samaritan*
in three views: approaching, broadside, and departing. The painting
is attributed to a British artist, R. B. Spencer, but the ship itself was the
last one built by the Bath firm of Clark & Sewall, which closed in
1855. A scene of great violence is projected by a hinter-glass painting
of *The Brig Caledonia in a Storm* (built 1828), by the Antwerp artist
Petrus Weyts.

A "please touch" room, with ship's wheel and bell, is popular with
children.

According to the *New York Marine Journal* (1891), "A Bath man
can no more help building ships than he can help breathing; and a
Bath man when he isn't building ships, sails them." By 1900 Bath had
produced half of the large wooden vessels sailing under the American
flag. During the Second World War the Bath Iron Works built more
destroyers than the entire Japanese navy.

The Maritime Museum administers three additional sites. The Winter
Street Center, at 880 Washington Street, a former church, is used as a
working center for the museum's staff and for changing exhibitions of
seafaring life. The riverside Apprenticeshop, at 375 Front Street, offers
an eighteen-month training program in constructing models, boat
building, and seamanship. The Percy and Small Shipyard, well down
the Kennebec River at 263 Washington Street, is the only surviving
shipyard in America of those that built large wooden sailing vessels.

An additional attraction is the unique steam tug *Seguin*, the oldest
U.S.-registered wooden steam vessel. Her restoration and new ship-house
are open for public inspection.

Bowdoin College Museum of Art

Location: Walker Art Building
Hours: September-June: Tues.-Fri. 10-4, Sat. 10-5; July and
August: Tues.-Sat. 10-5, Sun. 2-5; closed Mon. and holidays
Admission: Free. Ⓗ

An art collection has existed at Bowdoin almost since the inception of
the college itself. The earliest acquisition of major importance was a
group of 142 Old Master drawings bequeathed in 1811 by the Honorable James Bowdoin III, son of a governor of Massachusetts, and
himself a U.S. minister to France and Spain. Among many treasures—
appraised at the time for $7.50 the lot—this bequest contains a superb
pen-and-ink landscape by Pieter Brueghel the Elder. The collection
was the first of its kind in America. James Bowdoin III's Old Master
paintings came to the college two years later, in 1813.

Although various portions of the college's art collection were on
view during the first half of the nineteenth century, it was not until 1855
that a special gallery devoted to them came into being in the college
chapel. This was made possible by a gift from Theophilus Wheeler
Walker, a cousin of Bowdoin President Leonard Woods. As a memorial
to Walker his two nieces, Harriet Sarah and Mary Sophia Walker,
donated funds in 1891 for the erection of the present museum building,
designed by Charles Follen McKim of McKim, Mead & White. Four
tympana murals of *Athens, Rome, Florence,* and *Venice* by John
La Farge, Elihu Vedder, Abbott Thayer, and Kenyon Cox, respectively,
decorate the museum's Sculpture Hall.

The museum contains one of the most important collections extant
of American Colonial and Federal portraits, including works by Smibert,
Feke, Blackburn, Copley, Stuart, Trumbull, and Sully. Among the five
examples of Robert Feke's work is the full-length likeness of *General
Samuel Waldo,* generally regarded as among the finest American
portraits of the first half of the eighteenth century. Nine works by
Gilbert Stuart include the so-called official portrait of *Thomas Jefferson,*
as well as its pendant, *James Madison.* A complete catalogue of this
collection, *Colonial and Federal Portraits at Bowdoin College,* by
Marvin S. Sadek, was published in 1966.

The holdings in Ancient art include sculpture, pottery, bronzes, gems,
coins, and glass of all phases of the Ancient world. The most notable
benefactor in this area was Edward Perry Warren, the leading collector
of classical antiquities of the first quarter of the twentieth century. Five
magnificent ninth-century B.C. Assyrian reliefs from the Palace of
Ashurnazirpal II, the gift to the college of Henri Byron Haskell,
Medical 1855, are installed in the museum's Sculpture Hall. *Ancient
Art in Bowdoin College,* by Kevin Herbert, a descriptive catalogue, was
published in 1964 by the Harvard University Press.

In recent years, the college has been the recipient of a Samuel H. Kress Study Collection of twelve Renaissance paintings; a large collection of medals and plaquettes presented by Amanda, Marquesa Molinari; a fine group of European and American pictures given by Mr. and Mrs. John H. Halford; a collection of Chinese and Korean ceramics given by Governor and Mrs. William Tudor Gardiner; and 19 paintings and 168 prints by John Sloan bequeathed by George Otis Hamlin.

In the fall of 1964, the college was the recipient of the major portion of a collection of Winslow Homer memorabilia, which until that time had been in the artist's studio at Prout's Neck. This material, the gift of the Homer family, and now known as the Homer Collection of the Bowdoin College Museum of Art, includes the artist's first watercolor, a significant group of letters he wrote over a period of many years to various members of his family, and a considerable number of photographs of Homer, his family, and of Prout's Neck. More recently, a large group of woodblock reproductions of Homer's drawings that appeared in *Harper's* magazine was purchased to augment these holdings and create a major center for the scholarly study of Homer's life and work. The museum already owned a significant number of Homer's oils, watercolors, and drawings.

Other nineteenth-century American painters well represented here are Eastman Johnson, Thomas Eakins, George Inness, and Martin J. Heade; while for the twentieth century—in addition to the large collection of the work of John Sloan—William Glackens, Marsden Hartley, Andrew Wyeth, and Leonard Baskin are shown to advantage.

The museum is active in well-displayed temporary exhibitions, accompanied by scholarly catalogues meticulously designed. The Bowdoin College Traveling Print Collection is made available gratis to educational institutions in Maine. The museum also sponsors symposia and special lectures. Since 1973, symposia on American furniture, nineteenth-century decorative arts, American Indian art, nineteenth-century American architects, and conservation have been held.

Exhibition space in the Walker Art Building was more than doubled following an extensive renovation made possible by gifts to the 175th Anniversary Campaign Program and completed in 1976. Three galleries for exhibiting the museum's permanent collections and a temporary-exhibition gallery were added on the lower levels, and the previously existing galleries on the ground level were redecorated.

A handbook of the collections nears completion as of this writing.

McKim's masterly building (a Palladian adaptation of Brunelleschi's Pazzi Chapel in Florence), the impressive and wide-ranging holdings that we have outlined, and the sensitive taste of a series of directors have combined to make this the leading art museum in the state of Maine. Ambitious plans for the Portland Museum of Art may eventually make this statement obsolete, but certainly not in any near future. There is no visible abundance of James Bowdoin IIIs or of Edward Perry Warrens.

The five Assyrian reliefs, one of the larger groups received in the 1850s by New England colleges, primarily from missionary alumni serving at Mosul on the Tigris, are similar to those at Dartmouth,

Harvard, Middlebury, the University of Vermont, Williams, and Yale. We discuss them in the entry on Amherst College (MA 1)—because of its alphabetical priority and because it owns six.

Mr. Warren, the distinguished connoisseur who was Bowdoin's great benefactor in the field of Greek and Roman art, also contributed to the early development of the classical departments of the Boston Museum of Fine Arts and the Metropolitan Museum of Art in New York. From Bowdoin's Warren collection of Greek vases we have selected three Attic examples of quality to illustrate three methods of applying decoration to the clay surface, and to give some idea of stylistic range from the beginning of the fifth century B.C. to a high point of achievement at the middle of the century. (In architecture and architectural sculpture the same span would take us from the late Archaic temple at Aegina to the Temple of Zeus at Olympia.)

In the small *Black-figure Lekythos*,[1] an oil jar about 8 inches high dating from c. 490, the two foot soldiers were painted directly on the red clay in black silhouette, but their internal contour lines had to be laboriously scratched through the film of paint to reveal the red under-surface. This method had dominated most vase painting during the sixth century; but about 525 B.C. a much less confining process began to gain acceptance. It is seen in the *Red-figure Hydria*,[2] a three-handled water jar twice the height of the *lekythos* and dating from c. 460–450. Here the figures were drawn, both in outlines and in interior contour lines, and the background was then filled in with flat black paint. (A comparable reversal of an earlier process to gain greater freedom can be seen in the development of medieval enamels from Byzantine cloisonné to French champlevé as practiced during the thirteenth century at Limoges.) A third method, which brought vase painting still closer to what we think of as normal painting procedure, is seen in the *White-ground Lekythos*,[3] about 10 inches high and dating from c. 450. Here the entire vase was given a white slip, and then the artist drew and painted—as on a gesso panel or a canvas sized white—as he pleased. The second of the three methods eliminated the necessity of scratching lines through previously applied paint; the third avoided the difficulty of making the black background end exactly at the edges of the figures.

1

2

3

In its figure style, the *Black-figure Lekythos* recalls late sixth-century Archaic sculpture somewhat more than it does the relatively advanced sculpture of its own time, c. 490. Some Greek vase painters kept pace with sculptors in this voyage of anatomical discovery; others settled for accepted convention. An enormous advance in this direction is seen in the *Red-figure Hydria* of 460–450—but not without loss of ornamental appeal, for now something approaching an *independent picture* is wrapped around the vase. It is assigned to the Niobid Painter, one of the most skilled of his generation. Often such artists signed their names, but this one remains anonymous. In the case of the Niobid Painter, named after the subject of one of his major works in the Louvre, scholars have developed an impressive oeuvre. Here the subject is the rape of Oreithyia by Boreas as Athena watches and other figures flee from the scene. Greek painting was, of course, not limited to the ornamentation of vases, and leading fifth-century artists like Polygnotus are known to have made great wall paintings. It is very difficult to assign with any certainty connections between such masters and their modest counterparts who decorated vases, but scholars have succeeded in demonstrating that the Niobid Painter was indeed influenced by the art of Polygnotus himself. The *White-ground Lekythos* is assigned to the School of the Achilles Painter, one of the greatest figures of mid-fifth-century vase painting. But its quality by no means matches that of the master's works, for all its haunting charm. Such vessels, used frequently in burials, as frequently portray mourning persons like this man in a dull red himation before a stele and the woman on the reverse, offering red sashes.

In our concern with decoration we must not forget the vases themselves. Utilitarian objects, more often than not mass-produced (two hundred like our first illustration have been assigned to the same workshop), they attain great elegance even in their shape. Attempts have been made to discover complex mathematical formulae controlling their subtle outlines; but, as Rhys Carpenter has pointed out, the simplistic diagrams used in the demonstration are misleading. We do not *see* vases this way. However that may be, shapes of vases developed in ways similar to the evolution of Greek architecture and figured sculpture and painting. The two *lekythoi*, several decades apart, offer an example. The earlier one is relatively wide; the later, suavely elongated. Even the two lips are strikingly different. In the same order we note a change from a shape very much like the bearing portion (*echinus*, or cushion) of an Archaic Doric capital to a shape so narrow and vertical that it is clearly liberated from dependence on any such architectural model. The lovely Greek *kylix* (drinking cup) seen in MA 169 also seems related to the Doric *echinus*, and its evolution closely follows the development from Archaic Doric temples to the Parthenon.

Among the sculptures in the Warren collection is a superb marble *Statuette of a Nude Youth*,[4] dating from the Hellenistic era. Only the torso remains, its front somewhat marred by erosion and chipping. The position of three fingers on the left hip indicates that the left arm was held akimbo. With the entire weight held on the right leg, the figure takes a pronounced S-curve, first seen in the fourth-century sculptures of Praxiteles and Lysippos. The refinement of the carving precludes any possibility that this is a Roman copy of Greek work. The Swedish sculptor Carl Milles once told me that he collected Greek marbles because of the magnificence of their backs. The visitor is advised to observe this example accordingly. The figure may have represented a satyr, Hermes, or Narcissus.

The marble *Portrait Head of the Emperor Antoninus Pius*[5] (A.D. 138–161) is widely regarded as perhaps the finest Roman portrait in America. The flesh has a fine sheen, contrasting well with the rough hair passages. The eyes, with iris and pupil incised, bring the marble to life, and about the mouth there is a highly individualized suggestion of hesitancy.

All of this makes a fascinating contrast with a thirteenth-century French Gothic limestone *Head of a King*[6] from no less a source than Chartres Cathedral. At 6½ inches in height, it is about half the size of the Roman example. This crowned head is no royal portrait, but a biblical personage. The abstracted eyes and generalized mouth reveal no inner personality. The features remain close to the surface, without the projections and shadows of the Roman portrait. The fine rhythms of the flowing hair and short beard are an exercise in abstract design. They frame a three-dimensional shape that could be described in simple geometric terms. The unknown artist's intention was clearly to make

4

5

6

this head relate directly to architecture built of the same limestone; and we may assume that the body reflected similar architectural restrictions.

The identification of this head with Chartres Cathedral was made by Brooks Stoddard, at the time a teacher of art history at the college who specialized in medieval art. Knowing the Bowdoin head well, and re-membering that Chartres had been suggested as its possible origin, he explored the crypt of the cathedral, where there are many fragments, especially of the screen (*jubé*) that once separated the choir from the nave. A headless draped figure seemed to have the same break as the Bowdoin head. Stoddard then had a cast made at Harvard of the Bowdoin head, took the cast to Chartres, and placed it on the headless figure. The fit was perfect.

Included in the gift of the Samuel H. Kress Study Collection is a small oil on canvas representing *Apollo and Daphne*.[7] Its companion, *Cupid and Apollo Disputing the Power of Their Arrows*, went to Bucknell College (Lewisburg, Penn.). Formerly attributed to Andrea del Sarto, they are now generally agreed to have been the work of his important pupil Jacopo Pontormo (1494–1557) at the time of his ap-prenticeship. In 1512 the Medici were reinstated in Florence, and the youthful Lorenzo and Giuliano—more famous for their tombs by Michelangelo than for the wisdom of their tenure—decided to dazzle the public with elaborate festivals including floats. Andrea del Sarto was a chief designer of them, and the ornamentation went in for readily intelligible symbolism. Both Medici organized companies of retainers; Giuliano's honored Lorenzo the Magnificent with one of three floats symbolizing the Ages of Man. This float, *The Triumph of Summer*, used the Apollo and Daphne myth to refer to the great Lorenzo, who had adopted the laurel as his own device. Daphne, it will be remembered, escaped the ardent Apollo by being transformed into a laurel tree. The unusually reduced color, black and white only—almost like a chiaroscuro drawing—was presumably dictated by the design of the float itself.

It was mentioned earlier that James Bowdoin's gift of drawings, so poorly thought of by the appraiser, contained a pen-and-ink sketch by

7

Pieter Brueghel the Elder (c. 1525–69). This *View of Waltersburg*,[8] a town at the headwaters of the Rhine, is inscribed "Waltersspurg," in the old spelling. Brueghel went to Italy in 1551, and this drawing presumably dates from that time, because Waltersburg is on the old route between Flanders and Italy. While Brueghel's paintings show the result of his study of Renaissance anatomy and perspective, it is clear that what most impressed him on his trip was the rugged Alpine scenery. There are many Brueghel drawings of this sort in European collections today. He used them for the landscape backgrounds in some of his most famous pictures. Why it so closely resembles Chinese landscape art is hard to explain, but Benjamin Rowland, Jr., spotted such a similarity long ago. In *Art in East and West* (Harvard University Press, 1934), he pointed out that, like the Chinese, Brueghel drew from memory—I interject that though the Bowdoin drawing represents Waltersburg it can almost be exchanged with his other Alpine views. He developed a vocabulary of shorthand strokes to suggest the structure of rocks and trees, as the Chinese did. Rowland's comparison, illustrated by his plates 33 and 34, is based on the Brueghel *Alpine Landscape* in the Fogg Art Museum at Harvard.

After Brueghel, the next great leap in Flemish painting was taken by Peter Paul Rubens (1577–1640). We have discussed Rubens in full Baroque magnificence in an oil panel for the Whitehall Palace ceiling (CT 52), and we shall meet him several times again; but at Bowdoin there is a surprising little gem of a pen drawing of about 1602–05, *Thisbe Committing Suicide*.[9] Less than 4 inches high, it belongs with five other studies for this figure on a sheet in the Louvre (illustrated by Julius S. Held, *Rubens: Selected Drawings*, London: Phaidon Publishers, 1959, vol. II, pl. 9). These rapid little preliminary sketches, probably executed during his early sojourn at the court of the Gonzaga at Mantua, show Rubens already well launched toward his virtual invention of Baroque form, whereas his paintings of the same period are cramped and stiffened.

Little is known about Robert Feke (1707–52) before 1741, when he painted the *Family of Isaac Royall* in Boston (owned by Harvard Law School), and even less is known about him after 1750. It is apparent,

8

9

however, that he was influenced by Smibert's stiffened variation on the English Baroque of Kneller. (Compare CT 74 at Yale.) Smibert's Baroque interests are represented at Bowdoin by his copies, made in Italy, of Tintoretto, Poussin, and Van Dyck, and by his *Portrait of the Reverend James McSparran* (1735). But Feke refined Smibert's meaty grossness in favor of polished surfaces, clean lines, and decorative beauty. Thus he became the true precursor of Copley.

The *Portrait of James Bowdoin II*,[10] painted in 1748, is one of five Feke portraits at Bowdoin, all of that year. If the full-length *Brigadier General Samuel Waldo* (8 feet high) outstrips the others (all 50 by 40 inches) in size, the *James Bowdoin II* equals it in quality, and may even surpass it. In color, James's rich brown coat is set against cold blues and blue greens, his yellow-trimmed glistening white silk vest guiding our eyes swiftly up to his face. In the companion portrait of his wife the brown and blue sequence is reversed, but the whites serve a similar directional purpose. An ardent patriot and near the end of his life a governor of Massachusetts, he was twenty-two when the portrait was painted, and his wife of that year was seventeen.

To the Americanized Baroque of Smibert and Feke we may contrast the Anglo-American Rococo of Joseph Blackburn, painter of the primly elegant double portrait of *Elizabeth Bowdoin Temple and James Bowdoin III as Children*.[11] In his early training in England, Blackburn seems to have been influenced chiefly by Thomas Hudson, the master of Sir Joshua Reynolds. (A work by Hudson at the University of Vermont is discussed, VT 4.) Blackburn arrived from Bermuda in 1754 and painted in Boston, Salem, Portsmouth, and Newport until he returned to England in 1763. To judge from the age of James Bowdoin III (born 1752), this picture dates from well into Blackburn's American period. We need only remind ourselves of exactly contemporary portraiture at the court of Louis XV by Boucher and Nattier, or of Gainsborough's early work (see CT 54) to judge how far Blackburn was removed from the fashionable Rococo trends. Still, it would be hard to deny that in the Bowdoin children he painted a portrayal as delicious as it is improbable.

There is no evidence for the suggestion that Blackburn returned to England because John Singleton Copley (1738–1815) gave him too

10

11

much competition. But that Copley continued the purer American vein of Feke can easily be seen in his superb *Portrait of Thomas Flucker,*[12] painted c. 1770. A rabid Tory, Flucker was the last Royal Secretary of the Province of Massachusetts. By his first marriage he was the brother-in-law of Governor James Bowdoin II; by his second, the son-in-law of General Waldo. He wears a gray coat with gold buttons. The head is modeled with great force, and the expression is remarkably penetrating, even by Copley's high standards. Copley's American period ended in 1774, when he went to England, never to return. Occasionally he rose to his earlier heights (the *Mrs. Seymour Fort* at the Wadsworth Atheneum, CT 25, is an English work), but on the whole he became just another rather good English painter.

Gilbert Stuart (1755–1828) studied in Edinburgh when he was seventeen and went to London when he was twenty. He worked there from 1775 to 1787, when debts drove him to Ireland, where he remained until 1792. Except for a brief period in his teens at Newport (where his Copley-inspired *Portrait of Benjamin Waterhouse* is; see RI 1), Stuart was obviously a product of European training. He returned to America in 1793. His mature style was an important factor in what is sometimes called the release of American painting from its provincialism. I reserve the right to believe that the price of this artistic ransom was rather steep. I think that American portraiture suffered a confusing European-inspired deviation about 1800, and was only brought back on the track by the George Caleb Binghams, the Winslow Homers, and the Thomas Eakinses of later generations.

Be that as it may, Stuart's *Seated Portrait of Thomas Jefferson,*[13] commissioned by James Bowdoin III in 1805, is one of those significant points of contact that link a great personage with a leading artist of his own day. When we realize that Jacques Louis David began to paint the *Coronation of Napoleon* in Paris in the same year, it becomes clear that Stuart clung to the tradition of Sir Joshua Reynolds and resisted the swing to Neoclassicism that dominated most painting and sculpture at the turn of the century. Stuart's is without question the "classic"

13

12

portrait of the great President. Nevertheless, his image is at variance
with Jefferson's well-known classical tastes, and with his equally strong
French leanings. It is a Georgian image, though Jefferson himself
deplored Georgian architecture and its decoration. If we therefore find
this famous picture rather un-American, despite the understandable
patriotic sentiment that has become attached to it, we certainly do not
minimize its quality as a portrait and as a work of art.

For James Bowdoin III, Stuart also painted (again in 1805 and in
48-by-40-inch size) a *Seated Portrait of James Madison.* Here the status
symbols such as the column are less emphatic, the pose more informal,
and the characterization more intense. In their brilliant displays of
scarlet drapery, chairs, and tablecloths the two presidential images make
a sumptuous pair.

Martin J. Heade (1819–1904), discussed in the entry on the Benton
Museum at Storrs, Conn. (CT 100), is represented at Bowdoin by a
less ominous and more typical example, *Newburyport Marshes: Passing
Storm*[14] (c. 1865–70 and 15 inches high). A serpentine stream leads
us in and there is the expected little fringe of trees at the distant
horizon. But here, long before Claude Monet appropriated them as a
major theme, are two haystacks, one in shadow, the other catching the
light from its left. A serene gentleness pervades the scene, which may
have been painted from sketches made on Plum Island, off Newburyport.
Unlike Monet, however, Heade did not work on his canvases out of
doors, nor did he fragment his haystacks with light. He painted tender
idylls, not symphonic color poems.

It is appropriate that Bowdoin and Colby, as colleges in the state of
Maine, should own fine works by Winslow Homer (1836–1910), for
his later career developed there. From the Bowdoin collection let us
look at a very unusual example. It is not the best from a critical point
of view (I should nominate a late watercolor, *End of the Hunt*, for this
distinction), but it is in some ways the most interesting. The *Fountains
at Night*[15] was painted in 1893 after Homer visited the World's

14

15

Columbian Exposition in Chicago. That makes its subject exceptional enough. Equally remarkable, however, is the fact that Homer painted it in oils using gray tones only. There exist many other monochrome studies by Homer, but usually in gouache. Bowdoin has one (*Wolf's Cove*, Quebec, 1895) and the Farnsworth Museum at Rockland has another. Homer's oil shows Frederick MacMonnies's fountain by electrical illumination and the Venetian gondolas that plied the lagoons of the "White City." Such a work helps us to understand how important Homer felt the neutral tones were when he painted a watercolor like *End of the Hunt.*

Of the four lunettes in the elegant entrance rotunda, *Athens*,[16] painted in 1898 by John La Farge (1835–1910), is richest in color. The blues run deep; a dozen years earlier La Farge had preceded Gauguin in imbibing the colors of the South Seas. He had always admired the great Venetians. A statuesque calm, befitting the occasion, prevails. The figures are almost sufficiently generalized to avoid the disturbing thought that Victorians are posing in make-believe Greek costume. La Farge was intimately associated with architects: McKim, of course, and also H. H. Richardson, who chose him to decorate the interior of Trinity Church, Boston, with murals and designs for stained glass. It was the monumental sculptor Augustus Saint-Gaudens who recommended him to McKim for the Bowdoin commission. Of La Farge his ardent admirer Henry Adams wrote that he "owned a mind complex enough to contrast against the commonplaces of American uniformity, and in the process had vastly perplexed most Americans who came in contact with it."

Soon after the turn of the century, painting in America reacted strongly against the high idealism of artists like La Farge and the high-society images of John Singer Sargent. The revolt was led by Robert Henri and included seven others: Glackens, Luks, Shinn, Davies, Prendergast, Lawson, and John Sloan (1871–1951). From Bowdoin's

16

important representation of Sloan's work we have selected *Sunday Afternoon in Union Square*,[17] painted in 1912—a year before the opening of the riotous Armory Show in New York. Another 1912 picture by Sloan, *Sunday: Women Drying Their Hair* (Addison Gallery of American Art, Andover) was exhibited there, uncomfortably jostled by works of the European avant-garde. Sloan learned much from the competition, and applied it in his later painting. But in 1912 he was very much the Impressionist, sunlighting his bright colors and spicing his everyday images with an American's sharp observation of detail.

A branch of the Bowdoin Museum commemorates two famous Arctic explorers (and Bowdoin alumni), Admirals Robert E. Peary and Donald B. MacMillan. The display is located on the first floor of Hubbard Hall, for many years the college library.

17

Treat Gallery, Bates College

Location: From the Maine Tpke., take exit 13, drive northwesterly through the town to the college campus. The gallery is on the ground floor of Pettigrew Hall
Hours: Mon.-Fri. 1-4:30 and 7-8, Sun. 2-5; summer hours Tues.-Sat. 1-4
Admission: Free. Ⓗ

The gallery has an active schedule of temporary exhibitions. Until present hopes for expanded quarters materialize, the permanent collection is only sporadically on display. It contains a small number of good paintings, including portraits by Gainsborough and Beechey, and a composition of Roman ruins by Panini (or a follower); nineteen prints by Mary Cassatt; and gouaches and crayons by Carl Sprinchorn (1887–1971). There are many nineteenth- and twentieth-century prints and photographs.

The chief attraction, however, is a collection of ninety-nine drawings and two small early oils by Marsden Hartley (1877–1943) given in 1951 by the artist's heirs. A catalogue of the drawings, prepared by William J. Mitchell, was published by the college in 1970. The gift was made in accordance with Hartley's wish. He was born in Lewiston and spent the first fifteen years of his life there. After study and work in Europe, especially Berlin (see CT 30), and intermittent travel elsewhere, he repeatedly returned to his native state, and in his final decade divided his time between Maine and New York City. For a very fine late oil, see MA 21.

Pallid Spring,[18] signed and dated 1909 and dedicated to the artist's sister, precedes his pioneering modernism. A poetic little Impressionist landscape, vigorously brushed with small strokes of thick paint, it has something of the patterned surface effect of Maurice Prendergast's oils of the same year (see CT 99). The glories of Hartley's color in later years are already in evidence here.

18

The drawings range from delicate pencil sketches of landscape to aggressive work in pen and litho crayon, and from c. 1913 (Berlin) to Hartley's death. *Seated Man with Wide Collar*,[19] in litho crayon c. 1938/9, is typical of his latest phase. The bequest also includes many photographs of Hartley and his friends.

19

Museum of Art of Ogunquit

Location: Approach Ogunquit by Route 1; the museum is 1.4 miles south of Ogunquit Square on Shore Rd. Parking available
Hours: July through Labor Day, Mon.-Sat. 10:30-5, Sun. 1:30-5
Admission: Free

The museum, built in memory of Charles Godfrey Strater and Adeline Helme Strater, was completed in 1953. Constructed of cinder blocks and granite on three levels sloping down to the sea, it serves as a cultural center for the area. The collection is restricted to American art, with emphasis on recent painting, sculpture, graphic arts, and ceramics. Each summer there is a major temporary exhibition, usually based on the permanent holdings but supplemented by loans from elsewhere. These include broad surveys and one-artist shows. The museum owns fine examples of such painters as Bacon, Brook, Burchfield, Demuth, Hartley, Homer, Karfiol, Kuhn, Kuniyoshi, Luks, Marin, Marsh, Wyeth, and the founder, Henry Strater; and sculptures by Greenbaum, Lachaise, Zorach, and the ceramist Carl Walters.

One of the phenomena of modern art has been the decline of importance of the human figure as a subject. Abstract form is not, however, the only artistic alternative in a world beset by superhuman forces. A number of recent artists have found symbolic images in the animal and the bird kingdoms. The Ogunquit Museum allows us to compare two very different uses of the bird image. The sculptor John Flannagan (1895–1942) has expressed in *Pelican*[20] (1931) a timeless essence much in the character of ancient Egyptian art. Morris Graves (born 1910) has brushed *Bird with Spirit Mask*[21] (1953) with the magic of the Sung painters of ancient China. Both are modern in their emphasis on the fragment: Flannagan's bird is deliberately broken, while Graves's, its identity masked, is but an evocation. Flannagan found certainty in the durability of sandstone; Graves, in a world of spirit beyond the world of appearance. It is worth knowing that Flannagan carved *Pelican* during a year's stay in Ireland, where the rugged forms of the great

21

20

stone crosses made a lasting impression on him, and that Graves comes from the Pacific Northwest, whose museums are rich in Far Eastern art. Graves went to Ireland, too, in 1955/6, but the Ireland that interested him was another Ireland, one of mist-laden landscape.

Our final selection is by Mark Tobey (1890–1976). Though he came from Wisconsin and trained in Chicago, Tobey had, like Graves, a long association with the Pacific Northwest. After 1922 he lived in Seattle, but traveled to France, England, and the Far East, where he studied calligraphy and Zen. He eagerly absorbed Chinese and Persian philosophies stressing the unity of man and nature. *Meditative Series, Number 7*,[22] painted in tempera in 1954, may seem a meaningless labyrinth. It is indeed one, but so are the heavens on a moonless night. "Among and floating free above matted grasses, delicate threadlike structures rise and float . . . wind blown as the summer passes." This is a characteristic statement by Tobey; it may provide some bearings for his voyages into the infinite—all, in our example, at a size of only 18 by 12 inches.

In 1958 Tobey became the first American artist since Whistler (in 1895) to win first prize at the Venice Biennale. Three years later his European reputation was such that the Musée des Arts Decoratifs (in the Louvre) gave him a one-man exhibition of 286 works. Paris had given Whistler such a retrospective, at the Ecole des Beaux-Arts in 1905—two years after his death. Since that time no other American artist had been so honored—and Tobey still had fifteen years left him. In 1962 the Museum of Modern Art in New York energized lagging American acclaim with a retrospective of 135 works. It was also shown in Cleveland and Chicago.

22

The University of Maine Art Collection

Location: On the Penobscot River, about 15 miles north of Bangor
Hours: Open daily (but see below)
Admission: Free. Ⓗ

Since the university's large collection is placed in various public areas around the campus, the visitor should inquire at the curator's office in Carnegie Hall about the specific location of items. An illustrated catalogue is available there, without charge. Those concerned about security are reassured that proper vigilance is enforced.

The collection is primarily devoted to American art but it includes examples from abroad to assist in the teaching program. The print collection is extensive in the modern American field; it is supplemented by representative works by European masters from Dürer to Picasso. There are paintings of the Barbizon School here (Daubigny, Diaz) and one by Bouguereau (see MA 257). Among the Americans, Marsden Hartley, Childe Hassam, George Inness, William Kienbusch, John Marin, Waldo Pierce, Carl Sprinchorn, Abbot Thayer, and Andrew Wyeth are represented by oils, watercolors, or drawings. The most impressive sculpture is a bronze relief, *Awakening*, by the New York artist William Zorach, who spent much time working in Maine.

The Elm,[23] an oil by George Inness (1825–94), signed and dated 1864 and 3 feet high, is a serene and accomplished example of his early phase, in the vein of the Hudson River painters. We discuss Inness's further development in the 1870s as seen in works at Andover (MA 16) and Mount Holyoke College (MA 206).

23

A Bit of Cape Split,[24] signed and dated 1940, is one of two watercolors by John Marin (1870–1953) owned by the university. Marin's earlier career is discussed in examples at Waterville, Maine, and Rockland, Maine, and at Williamstown, Mass. (MA 275); the Orono selection carries his shorthand vocabulary almost to the point of Chinese calligraphy. As for color, only black and greenish grays are allowed to compete with the azures of Maine waters. Cape Split, the easternmost point in the United States, was "nearer his heart than any place in the world," according to Mackinley Helm, Marin's biographer. Like Winslow Homer before him, Marin found an escape on the lonely Maine coast—at Cape Split, Pleasant Bay, Schoodic Point, and Deer Isle. To find one in an earlier day, Homer had to venture only as far as Prout's Neck, below Portland.

24

Portland Museum of Art

Location: 111 High St. (corner of Spring St.); from Route 295 turn right on Forest Ave.; follow it to Congress St. (dead end), left to Oak St., then right on Spring St.

Hours: Tues.-Sat. 10-5, Sun. 2-5; closed Mon. and holidays

Admission: Free. Ⓗ projected

The museum was founded in 1882 as part of the Portland Society of Art, which also governs the Portland School of Art, founded in 1911. Its first permanent home came in 1908 through the bequest of Mrs. Lorenzo di Medici Sweat in memory of her husband, citizen of Portland and member of Congress. She left her home, erected in 1800 and now a Registered National Landmark, and funds for the construction of a gallery wing, opened in 1911.

The house itself is an exceptionally beautiful example of the Federal style. It was built by John Kimball, a local housewright, for Major and Mrs. Hugh McLellan. Its neighbor on Spring Street, the Charles Quincy Clapp House, built in 1832, and the McLellan-Sweat House itself form a distinguished island of historic New England architecture in a modern commercial city.

As of this writing, the museum is planning an ambitious expansion into a fifty-four-thousand-square-foot addition beyond the gallery wing and fronting on Congress Square. Designed by I. M. Pei & Partners, the architects of the already celebrated East Wing of the National Gallery of Art in Washington, it will bring the museum complex very much up to date. As always happens in such bold architectural ventures, there are shouts of joy and cries of protest; but if the Washington case is any parallel this will eventually settle down to a condition of municipal pride. The new building itself should stimulate future growth toward realization of the museum's goal of becoming Maine's chief cultural resource.

The museum displays works by Winslow Homer, the state of Maine collection, decorative arts, and temporary exhibitions; and it offers a full range of educational programs. The permanent holdings focus on the works of artists with Maine associations. Recently announced is a gift from Mr. Charles Shipman Payson of seventeen paintings by Winslow Homer ranging from 1868 to 1897. The Hamilton Easter Field collection, the gift of the Barn Gallery Associates in Ogunquit, includes among fifty-three works paintings by Bacon, Bouché, Davis, Field, Hartley, Karfiol, Kuhn, Kuniyoshi, Pascin, Spencer, Sterne, and von Schlegell; and sculptures by Gross and Laurent.

Other artists represented in the permanent collection include Arp, Badger, Brewster, A. B. Davies, Harding, Henri, Lachaise, Marsh, Motherwell, Nevelson, Prior, Renoir, Rivers, Steinberg, Frank Stella, Stuart, Whistler, Wyeth, and Zorach.

New York–Paris Number 2,[25] an oil 30 by 40 inches, was painted by Stuart Davis (1894–1964) in 1931. His early training under Robert Henri (see MA 207) directed him toward the social-realist themes of the so-called Ashcan School. Soon he turned toward modern abstraction but not until three or four years had elapsed since the Armory Show of 1913. By the time of Davis's year-and-a-half stay in Paris, in 1928/9, his work was already well advanced in the new direction, but the Paris experience gave him further confidence. The Portland example, painted eighteen months after his return to New York, shows how important it was to him. During the Depression years, Davis painted many murals under subsidy by the federal government. Other commissions included a mural for the men's lounge of Radio City Music Hall (1932), appropriately titled *Men without Women*; recently cleaned, it is still *in situ*. In 1978 the Brooklyn Museum organized a major retrospective of his work; the catalogue, by John R. Lane, is the most important study of many devoted to this important American artist.

25

The Joan Whitney Payson Gallery of Art, Westbrook College

Location: Take exit 8 from I-95 onto Route 25; go east about 1 ½ miles to Stephens Ave., turn left and follow to the college. Free parking

Hours: Tues.-Sat. 10-4, Sun. 2-5

Admission: Free

The collection of twenty-eight paintings and drawings formed by Mrs. Payson came to Westbrook College as the gift, in her memory, of her son John and his wife Nancy, an alumna and trustee of the college. They also gave the fine little cubic building, designed by The Architects Collaborative of Cambridge, in which it is so tastefully housed. The gallery opened to the public in 1977. Thus art in Portland is, so to speak, bounded by Payson donations—Mrs. Payson's collection at its west end and the massive contributions of her husband, Charles Shipman Payson, to the Museum of Art in the old city to the east.

The pictures are displayed on the ground floor and around a little balcony overlooking it. In the basement there is space for small temporary exhibitions. Most of the works are of good to very fine quality, and one masterpiece, Vincent van Gogh's *Iris*, is unforgettable. Even a list of the artists represented should whet the appetite: Chagall, Courbet, Daumier, Degas, Gauguin, Glackens, Homer, Ingres, Marquet, Monet, Picasso, Prendergast, Renoir, Reynolds, Rousseau-le-douanier, Sargent, Sisley, Soutine, van Gogh, Whistler, and Wyeth. We illustrate and discuss four of them and regret that space precludes the inclusion of more. Unfortunately, too, the great Courbet, *Stormy Weather at Etretat*, does not photograph well in black and white. I should like to have compared it with Homer's imposing but less potent marine, *The Backrush* (close by), painted at Prout's Neck at least twenty years later, in order to commit a pun for which I hope I shall be forgiven: that Courbet's vision was the more Homeric.

In *A Painter*,[26] a drawing in crayon, pen, and wash, Honoré Daumier (1808–79) is seen in his late, free phase. For contrast, see the early lithograph of 1834, CT 41. Highly sculptural contour lines now re-

26

place the former laborious modeling in light and shade, and subtle washes of shadow reinforce them. Darker washes plunge the image into a Rembrandtesque gloom. In his oils, few of which date from before 1850, Daumier adopted a technique much like this.

Little need be said about Vincent van Gogh's *Iris*[27] except that it was painted in the spring of 1889 at Saint-Remy in Provence, a full year later than his pen-and-ink *View of Arles*, now in Providence (RI 20). Masterpieces have a way of being self-explanatory. You will not overlook the spiked rhythms of the green leaves, repeated or introduced in the orange-red foreground, or the variant greens at the top of the canvas, or the shrill contrast between blue and orange blossoms, or the single white blossom at the left—somehow suggesting a woman's bonnet. Is this really a flower piece, or is it an allegory of the human condition?

Jungle with Monkeys,[28] by Henri Rousseau (1844–1910), painted in 1909, has the scary big scale, although it is only 2 feet high, and the harsh color contrast of his latest work, as well as the power of his very large pictures. New England has few examples by this mysterious, mostly self-taught artist. It is surprising to realize that he was a contemporary of the Impressionists, from whom he differed so markedly. (Compare the oranges with Renoir's onions, for example, in the Clark Institute's picture, MA 256.) A modest customs agent (*douanier*), Rousseau painted at off hours and then indulged in it full time; but he attracted little notice until the avant-garde discovered him. A big jungle painting of Rousseau's hung in the main gallery of the anti-Salon (of the Independents) in 1905 along with works by the Fauves. In 1908 he was the guest of honor at a strenuous banquet staged by Picasso and attended by Apollinaire, Georges Braque, Gertrude and Leo Stein, Alice Toklas, Marie Laurencin, Maurice Vlaminck, and many others. For further details, see Roger Shattuck's fascinating volume, *The Banquet Years* (Garden City, N.Y.: Anchor Books, 1961).

If you can manage to attend a concert without knowing what the program will be, you are sure to listen with the greatest concentration and learn much from the experience. (Is this really by Mozart, or is it

27

28

Haydn, or a minor contemporary?) In the same way, I suggest you look at *Road Cut*[29]—whether in the original or in our illustration—before reading further. If you are actually visiting the Payson Gallery don't look at the illustration, because it is the color of this picture that gives it much of its powerful expression. Go to the original! Even though the painter is well known to you, you may be in for a surprise, as I was. The brittle tempera medium, the harsh wiry lines, the bare tree, the stark loneliness—these ring bells in the memory. But these deep russets, close to the color of red wine? If you are on the right track, you expect only sepia browns, blacks and grays, pale acid greens and sooted bleached yellows. The following information may or may not help: the picture was painted in 1940 when the artist was only twenty-three. Nearby is another of his works, *The Chair*, a dry-brush painting on paper, a minor but fully typical example of his developed style. Now I suspect you know who he is. But if so, a question remains. Did he develop significantly from his marvelous beginnings? An answer to this question is suggested in our discussion of a major work of the artist's later years, at the Shelburne museum (VT 25).

29

William A. Farnsworth Library and Art Museum

Location: On Route 1 (Main St.), turn west on Museum St. There is a parking lot at the Union St. end of the block

Hours: June 1-September 30: Mon.-Sat. 10-5, Sun. 1-5; October 1-May 31: Tues.-Sat. 10-5, Sun. 1-5. Closed legal holidays. The homestead is open only June 1 to mid-September, at the same hours as the library and museum

Admission: Free

In accordance with the will of Lucy C. Farnsworth, of Rockland, the museum, completed in 1948 as a memorial to her father, has become a cultural and educational center for the Penobscot area. The nationally registered Farnsworth Homestead, built in the Greek Revival style of the first half of the nineteenth century, stands on the adjacent property. The house, with its interior furnished in the Victorian style, is maintained exactly as when the Farnsworths occupied it.

The Farnsworth Library, handsomely appointed, is a rich source for the study of Maine history, maritime life, and art history. The permanent collection of the museum specializes in American paintings, drawings, and prints of the eighteenth century to the present. A complete catalogue of them was published in 1975. European and Oriental art are also represented.

In the summer season the museum often stages a major exhibition of the work of an artist with Maine associations. Two of the most memorable were devoted to Fitz Hugh Lane (see MA 155), who often painted scenes of Rockland harbor, and Louise Nevelson (see MA 147), whose early years were spent in Rockland. Since these exhibitions sometimes occupy most of the available gallery space, visitors who wish to see the permanent collection should take that into consideration.

In addition to the four painters discussed below, other prominent Americans represented here include Washington Allston, Thomas Eakins (small oil studies for *William Rush Carving the Nymph of the Schuylkill* and *The Thinker*), William Harnett (a large still life of quality comparable to the example we discuss at Springfield, Mass.), Edward Hopper, William Jennys, Eastman Johnson, John F. Kensett, Fitz Hugh Lane (three oils and a drawing; see our discussion of his work at Gloucester Mass.), Maurice Prendergast, Gilbert Stuart, Thomas Sully, and the Wyeths—N.C., Andrew, and James—permanently displayed in an upstairs gallery.

Storm Clouds on the Coast,[30] an oil of 1859 by Martin J. Heade (1819–1904), is very different in mood from the summer idyll we have studied at Bowdoin College (ME 14); but it shares much in ominous immensity with the smaller *Rye Beach, New Hampshire* at the University of Connecticut (CT 100). Here the generous size (20 by 32 inches) gave Heade a more extended range. A rocky island and a sailboat, diminutive but crisply silhouetted, mark its outer limit. The approaching wave is no monster, yet its fringe has great energy.

A calm sea sets the mood for *A Girl in a Punt*,[31] a small gem of a watercolor by Winslow Homer (1836–1910). The freely brushed strokes, very liquid and transparent, accentuate a restful horizontality. The punt does not disturb it, nor does the sailboat, not far away. A foreground rock points toward the girl, but her oar blocks further passage off to the left. She is the darkest and the largest element in the picture, and inevitably she leans across the direction defined by the rock. Homer signed the picture but did not date it. A second watercolor, *Sailing Ships in Harbor*, in opaque white gouache on brown paper, is signed and dated 1880. Comparison with a large number of watercolors and gouaches painted that summer at Gloucester, Mass., suggests that *Girl in a Punt* also dates from that year. Compared with Homer's earliest watercolors of the mid-1870s, there is now a larger scale, a more liquid wash, greater freedom in the use of the medium, and a darkening color and atmosphere. There are only two oils of 1880 (one a beach scene in the Springfield Museum), and they too are sunless and serious. All of this, we should not forget, was produced before Homer went to England in 1881 and changed his basic theme into one of the struggle of man against the sea.

The schooner in our next picture is in dangerous waters. The scene is off the great cliffs of Monhegan Island, the date is September 1913, and the artist is George Bellows (1882–1925). *Boating out to Sea*[32] is one of three of his oils owned by the Farnsworth Museum. *Autumn— Camden*, twice as large, is more typical, but it lacks the concentrated power of our selection. Lowering color and vigorous brushwork underlie the ominous impact.

30

31

32

Marine Landscape,[33] a watercolor by John Marin (1870–1953), is an offbeat masterpiece. The tenderly applied washes recall Marin's work of around 1910–13 (see ME 38); there is virtually no evidence of the harsh, jagged strokes that mark his watercolors of around 1920. This example was painted in 1919, as the abbreviated signature makes clear. The colors are gentle too, and that is most exceptional. They are like a Whistlerian symphony in pale pastels. Yet behind this delicate surface lies a firm, rectangular structure, not found in the early watercolors; and the scale has Marin's mature boldness. What one normally expects from him can be seen in the smashing example at Williams College (MA 275).

In addition to the artists listed or discussed above, the Farnsworth Museum offers an opportunity to study the work of lesser but talented masters. Three ship painters deserve close attention: James Baldridge, Robert Salmon (five oils here, from 1822 to 1832), and William Stubbs. Do not miss the examples by Frank Benson (see MA 168), Alfred Bricher (see MA 161), Charles Codman, Alvan and Jonathan Fisher, Waldo Pierce, and Paul Sample.

33

Dyer-York Library and Museum

Location: Main St. (Route 1) at intersection of North St.; from Maine Tpke. take exit 5
Hours: In summer, Tues.-Sat 1-4; in winter, Tues. and Thurs. 10-4, Sat. 1-4
Admission: Free

The York Institute Museum was incorporated in 1867; its present home was erected in 1926 and a gallery wing was added in 1968. The neighboring Dyer Library, including a well-equipped research center, occupies the remodeled former home of the Deering family.

The front portion of the museum contains a Colonial kitchen, Empire and eighteenth-century bedrooms, and furnishings and artifacts from the family of Colonel Thomas Cutts, Saco's great landowner and shipbuilder of the Revolutionary period. Those interested in the genre plaster groups of John Rogers, mid-nineteenth century, will find some twenty examples. Of special local interest is a small oil painting of an Anti-Slavery meeting at the old Gibbs Hotel by Charles H. Granger, a Saco artist.

In connection with Smibert's full-length *Portrait of Sir William Pepperrell* at Salem (MA 196), it is interesting to find, at Saco, silver presented to him by Commodore Peter Warren, whose British squadron assisted Pepperrell's force of 4,240 New England farmers and tradesmen in taking the French fortress of Louisburg. That was in 1745, and all these fine pieces bear hallmarks for the same date. Such was the hurry on Warren's part to make this presentation in the year of the victory that each piece was made by a different craftsman, and the pineapples in the Pepperrell shield were inadvertently reversed. The two large double-handled and covered cups are particularly magnificent.

From the point of view of the scope of this book, however, the greatest treasure here is a group of thirteen portraits by John Brewster, Jr. (1766–1854), a deaf-mute itinerant painter born in Connecticut. We have discussed a portrait of his at the Connecticut Historical Society (CT 7), and now refer the reader to articles on Brewster in that society's *Bulletin* for October 1960, and in *Antiques* for November of that year. The York Institute has published a small brochure on the artist's remarkable career. Apparently he spent several months about 1800 at the Cutts mansion in Saco and painted the whole family. Not surprisingly, the largest pictures are the full-length ones of Colonel Cutts himself and of his wife Elizabeth. The *Portrait of Colonel Cutts*[34] (1736–1821), aged about sixty-five, may be described as a stiffened American Holbein. Black and white dominate this stark icon. Everything is rigidly vertical except the colonel's fingers, crossing exactly at right angles the black-and-white diagonal of his cane. How the cane stays put is not revealed, but where in painting is there a diagonal more incontrovertible?

In 1980 the portraits of Colonel and Mrs. Cutts traveled to a major exhibition of American folk painting at the Whitney Museum of American Art, New York.

34

Penobscot Marine Museum

Location: Church St., just off Route 1
Hours: Open Memorial Day weekend through October 15, Mon.-Sat. 9:30-5, Sun. 1-4
Admission: Charged

Marine museums are fascinating places and art is no stranger to them. To our entries on those at Bath and, in other states, Mystic, New Bedford, and Salem, we are happy to add this account of six neighboring houses in a charming village at the head of Penobscot Bay.

The museum was incorporated in 1936, when Searsport presented to the trustees its original Town Hall, built in 1845 from funds given by David Sears of Boston, the town's eponym. Purchase and restoration of "the Captain's House," the former home of Captain Jeremiah Merithew (c. 1816), facilitated the exhibition of a rapidly growing collection relating to Maine shipping and coastal life. Four other buildings provide quarters for special exhibitions, a small craft exhibit, workshops, and an intimate presentation of life at Searsport in times long gone. The main displays, in the Old Town Hall and the Captain's House, show the same taste and expertise that mark the Maine Maritime Museum at Bath. A research library is one of the features of the Captain's House, along with displays of furniture, glass, ship models (including the *Charles W. Morgan*, the original of which can be visited at Mystic Seaport), memorabilia of the China Trade, and large eighteenth-century panels depicting various phases of whaling. The Old Town Hall features half-size models of Maine-built ships and ship portraits. The collection of marine paintings, shown throughout the complex, is regarded as one of the finest in the state.

Gerald Brace, my favorite writer on Maine, sums it all up toward the end of *Between Wind and Water* (Norton, 1966): "The people on the old coast of Maine were not romantic philosophers or poets—they were not at all bookish or self-conscious—but they did seem to provide the evidence on which philosophy could build. They illustrated what could be done when the right people and the right place and climate and conditions all collaborated in a harmonious and at best beautiful way of life." On page 67 you can find out why "nor'west" and "sou'west" are correct, and why "nor'east" and "sou'east" will instantly betray you as an ignoramus.

Colby College Art Museum

Location: From I-95 take the Waterville exit; the college is located on a hill to the west of the city
Hours: Mon.-Sat. 10-12, 1-4:30; Sun. 2-4:30; closed holidays
Admission: Free

With the opening in 1959 of the Bixler Art and Music Center, Colby's already important art collection was at long last appropriately housed. The new building immediately stimulated enthusiastic support from the Friends of Art at Colby and impressive donations. Like all college museums, Colby's is indispensable for the teaching of art history and studio courses. As of this writing, Colby College is the leading center for the study of advanced modern art in the conservative state of Maine. While the Ogunquit Museum shares that distinction, it is open only in the summer months.

The Colby collection, however, is by no means limited to the modern field. Its range extends from a large and fine group of Colonial and Federal portraits and nineteenth-century American folk art through major masters of the nineteenth century. While the emphasis here is on American art, Europeans from the Dutch seventeenth century, British portraits, and moderns like Utrillo, Kirchner, Klee, and Philip Guston are represented. Decorative arts are well represented too, notably by the Bernat collection of three hundred examples of Oriental ceramics. There are many fine drawings and prints.

As the only noncoastal art museum of significance in Maine, Colby's has attracted the interest of residents and artists with Waterville connections. (The important art school at Skowhegan is only twenty miles to the north.) The two most extensive of the earlier donations were the Helen Warren and Willard Howe Cummings collection of American paintings and folk art, and the American Heritage collection of American primitive paintings and drawings, the gift of Mr. and Mrs. Ellerton Jetté. Since 1949 a precious selection of the work of Winslow Homer has been on extended loan from Mrs. Harold T. Pulsifer. Mr. and Mrs. John Marin, Jr., have given twenty-five works by Mr. Marin's father, ranging from an 1888 watercolor to a 1952 oil. Two distinguished sculptors contributed: William Zorach gave a bronze of his well-known *Mother and Child*, and Louise Nevelson (see MA 147), twenty of her drawings, twelve small sculptures, and four paintings.

If our selections skip over the Early American portraits, that is because they are in such quantity in New England and we wish to emphasize more recent art here, for reasons given above. The collection has good examples of Smibert, Wollaston, Joseph Badger, McIlworth (see MA 174), Earl, Copley, Charles Willson Peale, and Gilbert Stuart; and among the anonymous portraits one of *The Reverend Silas Ilsley*, c. 1840, is outstanding.

We begin our survey with *Landscape with River and Temple*,[35] signed and dated 1773 by Richard Wilson (1714–82). A master rarely seen in New England museums, he was the virtual founder of British landscape painting. Until he was thirty-five he painted portraits; then he set out for Italy. There he remained about five years and mastered the landscape art of Claude Lorrain and Gaspard Poussin, with their dark foreground *coulisses* starting the viewer on a journey back into a distant light. On his return Wilson seems to have studied the Dutch landscape painters. In this late example we find an eighteenth-century flattening of the extreme spaciousness of his seventeenth-century models, and some lessening of their solidity. Irregularities like the scarred bark of the tree at the left and the picturesque cliff beyond it unsettle Claude's soft calm. While the scene is probably imaginary, it could pass as the depiction of a real place. Color and brushwork, held in restraint, await the Constables and Turners yet to come. As is well known, there was little demand for such pictures in Wilson's lifetime; recognition for his brave departure did not come until well after his death. At the end, he retired to his native Wales, a broken man.

Still-life painting had an enormous vogue in nineteenth-century America. Of many examples at Colby, *Still Life with Oranges*, by William J. McClosky, is memorable, but perhaps surpassed by *Still Life with Melons and Fruit*,[36] by Thomas Badger (1792–1868). The latter, no doubt influenced by similar assemblages by Raphaelle Peale, has produced a sumptuous dining-room ornament, given it a substantial pyramidal structure, and displayed a virtuoso's technique. Little details

35

36

like the spilled seeds from the watermelon did not escape his notice. For a later and still more elaborate production, compare the work of Severin Roesen (VT 6).

We have discussed an early oil by Winslow Homer (1836–1910) at Yale (CT 80) and a watercolor of 1880 at Rockland (ME 31), but at Colby we can study to advantage Homer's earliest ventures into the difficult watercolor medium. *The Berry Pickers*,[37] signed and dated July 1873, comes from the very first year he worked in watercolor. Though he was later to carry it to unheard-of marvels—such as *Three Men in a Boat*, 1890, also at Colby—this example, once seen, has a way of returning to the memory as one of his masterpieces. This despite a certain tightness and dependence on preliminary drawing, and on opaque white wash (gouache) to increase the solidities. Perhaps that very hesitancy contributes to the image's tender and nostalgic appeal. Henry James's reaction to such innocents has already been quoted; in the presence of *The Berry Pickers* it seems incomprehensible. But then, James recommended Algiers and Capri as proper subjects for painting.

Brooklyn Bridge,[38] a watercolor of 1912 by John Marin (1870–1953), is as loose and liquid as *The Berry Pickers* is taut and brittle. Curiously, Marin progressed in the opposite direction from that of Homer, as may be quickly seen here in a comparison with *Stonington*, a watercolor of 1925, or with the 1940 example discussed at Orono (ME 24). Painted a year before the Armory Show, *Brooklyn Bridge* precedes Marin's gradual absorption of European Cubism, with its interpenetrating planes, and Italian Futurism, with its angular collisions of industrial and urban forms. We marvel at how these little puddles

37

38

of color manage to shape a whole vista of Manhattan seen from the Brooklyn waterfront.

We continue with two landscapes, both street scenes and both painted between 1910 and 1916. Here the similarity ends, for the Childe Hassam (1859–1939) *View of Broadway: Newburgh, N.Y.*[39] has an American freshness and charm, while the Maurice Utrillo (1883–1955) *Street in Le Vésinet*[40] is weighted down with Old World cares in its leaden gray loneliness. In its company the Hassam, a watercolor, sparkles with optimism. The blue air and waters of the Hudson carry through the holiday mood set by the flags. Hassam often made hackneyed variations on the work of the French Impressionists. Here he stands on his own.

The Utrillo is an early oil from his best period (c. 1910). The design is tautly laced by the sharply receding planes. No breeze, no people animate this suburb. Eventually, Utrillo drank himself to death, and unlike two colleagues in alcoholism, Toulouse-Lautrec and Modigliani, he injured his artistic powers in the process. Toward the end, he tossed up repetitious confections based on tourist postcards. Utrillo's streets always lead in the same direction, and eventually they led him to a vacuum.

With *Agricultural Experimental Plan for Late Fall*,[41] a fantasy in watercolor and ink by Paul Klee (1879–1940), we truly enter the realm of modern art, despite its long-ago date in the 1920s. The title, inscribed in Klee's spidery hand, is his own; and it is our guarantee that this image is no pure abstraction. A master of line, shape, color, and space, Klee exploited the medium of painting at its purest to express profound ideas about life and death. This example is about life, and how to generate it; after the mid-1930s, when the Nazis came to power, he was concerned with death. Swiss-born, he worked primarily in Germany, and after 1920 at the celebrated Bauhaus until the Nazis dissolved it

39

41

40

in 1933. Ultimately he returned to his native Bern, to end his days there in deepest pessimism. But in the 1920s he was much affected by the architectural discipline of the Bauhaus exerted by its founder, the architect Walter Gropius, as was his Russian-born colleague Kandinsky (see CT 83). It is too easy to compare Klee's works of this period with intricate Swiss toys; but they do invoke a world of magic as if seen under a magnifying glass. Klee's paintings—all unrepetitive nine thousand of them—are little poems to personal privacy and to the freedom of the artist's imagination. That is why the Nazis declared his art "degenerate."

By Klee's standards, our next two American oils are obviously conservative, even though they date from the next decade, or later. It is surprising to discover that Walt Kuhn (1877–1949) was a near contemporary of Klee's; but the American concern with describing an image in readily understandable terms was not yet prepared to yield to European countertraditions. Thus for Kuhn the clown *Mario*[42] was the portrait of a man, and not, as for Rouault (see NH 28), a symbol of fragile existence on the edge of life. For all that, it is solidly painted, strongly designed, and expressively characterized. The date is 1938.

Shell and Feather,[43] by Georgia O'Keeffe (born 1887), might seem without its color a superb photograph of two objects sensitively selected and as sensitively arranged. But the aesthetic appeal of these whites and near whites and shell pinks is considerable, as is the controlled smooth brushwork. Set in a nowhere space, the objects tell us much about shapes we have seen but not really observed.

Colby's sculpture collection is small. The best examples are American primitive or modern. We conclude with two examples of the latter. Set

42

43

out of doors, *Stranger III*,[44] a bronze nearly 8 feet high, is a fine example of the work of the English artist Lynn Chadwick (born 1914). It is the gift of Jere Abbot, a former director of the Smith College Museum of Art celebrated for his eye for quality in modern art. Dating from 1957–59, this disquieting three-legged personage spreads its ominous wings under the flattened square of an inhuman head. In his brief monograph on the artist (Universe Books, 1961), the critic J. P. Hodin describes another piece in the *Stranger* series: "The animal form suggests the human, a metamorphosis which by way of a shock gives the beholder a sensation of the unprecedented. The transitoriness of all living substance, be it man, animal or plant, is suggested as well . . . although there is no primary intention to produce a series, a formal problem can show itself so interesting that it demands further investigation or formal exploitation until the fascination ebbs away."

Torso,[45] a ceramic sculpture 20 inches high, is the work of the Japanese-American Isamu Noguchi (born 1904). After responding to its powerful simplification and its formidable stance, you will not be surprised that Noguchi studied with Brancusi (see CT 68) in Paris, and became his assistant. That was in his youth, in 1927/8. This piece comes from thirty years later, when he had succeeded in fusing his Japanese heritage with the sculptural inventions of modern Western art. Note the importance of the straps that bind the hips, the subtly flattened rib cage and its transition to the abdomen—the very antithesis of explosive Baroque, and of Rodin. One nipple is simply a hole, informing you that the piece is only a shallow shell; but a hole is the opposite of a bulge, as Henry Moore has often pointed out, and hollows formed in rocks by the action of water are a potent form of sculpture in nature. Therefore, a hole is simply a bulge seen inside out.

44

45

Index

Numbers refer to pages, not illustrations. In longer entries only the first page is indicated.

The Art Museums of New England

was designed by Jean LeGwin and set in linotype Garamond, a face designed by Claude Garamond, who died in 1561. Garamond lived and worked at a time when black-letter fonts were in course of being superseded in France by types based on the Renaissance hands we now call roman and italic. He derived his inspiration from the Aldine old face, and the influence of his work dominated European typefounding for the succeeding two centuries. Many punches cut by other hands were subsequently ascribed to him, including the historical prototypes of many of the revivals bearing his name at the present time. The roman is based on fonts recorded as Garamond's work in specimens issued in Germany between 1592 and 1702, and its italics derives from originals ascribed to Robert Granjon of Lyons in the same specimens. Both series were the work of R. Hunter Middleton, and were issued in 1930.

THE ART MUSEUMS OF NEW ENGLAND was composed by Lamb's Printing Company, Clinton, Massachusetts and printed on Monadnock's Greenfield Opaque. Halliday Lithograph, West Hanover, Massachusetts was the printer and binder.